D0873996

Sometimes we're so busy serving Jesus that we fail to enjoy him. Or so preoccupied with the ministry of the Word, that we forget to commune with the Word made Flesh. **Pause with Jesus** rescues us from this cruel irony. With sparse, elegant prose, Chris Maxwell gives fresh glimpses of our Lord from the pages of Scripture. Maxwell's insights and images will encourage you to slow down and enjoy Jesus again—and then serve him out of love and wonder, not duty and shame.

— DREW DYCK
  MANAGING EDITOR OF *Leadership Journal*
  AUTHOR OF *Yawning at Tigers*

Pause with Jesus is an excellent addition to Chris Maxwell's series of "Pause" books. Thirty bite-sized chapters of just a few pages each invite readers to pause and meet Jesus—in poetry and prose, in Scripture, with questions, personal reflection, and practical responses. This is a great resource for individuals and groups to explore and deepen their relationship with Jesus. Thank you, Chris, for your words of blessing, encouragement, and inspiration.

— APRIL YAMASAKI
  LEAD PASTOR, EMMANUEL MENNONITE CHURCH, ABBOTSFORD, BC, CANADA
  AUTHOR OF *Sacred Pauses: Spiritual Practices for Personal Renewal*

Chris Maxell is a storyteller with the eyes of a poet and a pastor with the heart of a mystic. In this fourth installment of the "Pause" series, Chris chooses 30 scenes from the life of Christ and then invites you to hit pause and step into each story. Then he invites you to take the time to read, reflect, receive and respond, before you step back with Jesus into your life.

— GARY W. MOON, MDIV, PHD
  EXECUTIVE DIRECTOR MARTIN INSTITUTE AND DALLAS WILLARD CENTER, WESTMONT COLLEGE,
  AUTHOR OF *Apprenticeship with Jesus*

My friend Chris Maxwell always has a word in season. Every time Chris encourages me or prays with me, he seeks to bring the presence of Jesus into the storm I'm facing. This book will do the same for you. It will teach you to pause, breathe, let go of your fears, step out of your boat and grab hold of the Savior.

— J. LEE GRADY
    FORMER EDITOR, *Charisma Magazine*
    DIRECTOR, THE MORDECAI PROJECT

*Is it just me, or does Chris Maxwell get better with each paragraph he pens? Chris Maxwell's **Pause with Jesus** invites us to enter the narrative of the Gospels, place ourselves in the story, and experience the presence of Christ as never before. I found myself looking through the window into each scene one minute and beholding myself in a mirror the next. **Pause with Jesus** provides thirty robust opportunities to meet Jesus at the intersection of life and truth. Read it. Share it. Talk about it. Savor it. But don't get in a hurry.*

— C. TRACY REYNOLDS, DOCTOR OF STRATEGIC LEADERSHIP
    DEAN, SCHOOL OF CHRISTIAN MINISTRIES
    EMMANUEL COLLEGE

*How one could accomplish to tell the greatest story ever told in a fresh, new, and powerful way is beyond me. Yet, my dear friend, Chris Maxwell, has done just that. A true Ambassador for the kingdom of God and a representation of Christ's love demonstrated on earth, Chris has penned a tapestry of stories that reveal truth, inspire reflection, invite connection, and honor Christ's supremacy, deity, and humanity. **Pause with Jesus** displays the truth of a loving God who welcomes us from all walks of life to come into His presence and truly connect with their Savior, Redeemer, and Friend. I hope that everyone who reads this book accepts this heartfelt invitation to pause with Jesus. I am so glad I did.*

— CHEMELLE EVANS
    VICE PRESIDENT, SNOW COMPANIES

Pause with Jesus is more than just a book. It's a journey. Through his words, Chris is inviting us to slow down and listen for Christ's unmistakable voice, feel the gentle strength of His embrace, and see the timeless beauty of His work. The more you read the clearer you will see Jesus gazing back at you.

— MAX BARROSO
  DIRECTOR OF THE AWAKENING (IPHC MINISTRIES)

In an era when Jesus is being used, and abused, by so many to justify their own actions and attitudes, it is refreshing to read about Jesus in a way that leads us back to His words, His life, His call. Chris Maxwell, in this edition of his ongoing collection of writings under the phrase "Pause," has led us, like Mary in Luke 10:39, to the feet of Jesus.

— DR. A. D. BEACHAM
  GENERAL SUPERINTENDENT, INTERNATIONAL PENTECOSTAL
  HOLINESS CHURCH

*Reading through **Pause with Jesus**, I'm impressed … again. To say Chris Maxwell has a way with words is, well, an understatement. Words stimulate. Words motivate. Words hit home and make us think. Words encourage and comfort. And the words in **Pause with Jesus** do all this and more. This is another masterpiece in the "Pause" series. Thanks, Chris.*

— RON WHITE, EdD
  PRESIDENT, EMMANUEL COLLEGE

*The message in **Pause with Jesus** is the answer to every need, every care, every longing in our life. Thank you Chris Maxwell for "pausing" long enough to hear from God and write this treasure.*

— REBECCA KEENER
  PASTOR OF MARRIAGE MINISTRY, FREE CHAPEL
  CO-HOST, "THE CHRISTIAN VIEW"

PAUSE
WITH JESUS

*Encountering His Story
in Everyday Life*

CHRIS MAXWELL

True Potential
REACH THE WORLD

Chapter one is taken from *Unwrapping His Presence* by Chris Maxwell and published by Higher Life Publishing, Orlando, FL.

Chapter thirteen was originally published in *Montage* 2015, Emmanuel College, 15–18.

True Potential, Inc
PO Box 904
Travelers Rest, SC 29690
www.truepotentialmedia.com

PAUSE WITH JESUS
Encountering His Story in Everyday Life

ISBN: 978-1-943852-06-2 (paperback)
ISBN: 978-1-943852-07-9 (eBook)

Printed in the United States of America.

Other Books by Chris Maxwell

Beggars Can Be Chosen: An Inspirational Journey Through the Invitations of Jesus

Changing My Mind: A Journey of Disability and Joy

Unwrapping His Presence: What We Really Need for Christmas

Pause: The Secret to a Better Life, One Word at a Time

Pause for Moms: Finding Rest in a Too Busy World

Pause for Pastors: Finding Still Waters in the Storm of Ministry

A Table of Words

Thanks to So Many

Thank you. To so many people, I say thank you. For loving me, forgiving me, accepting me, believing in me, thank you.

To Debbie, Taylor, Aaron, and Graham, thank you. To daughters in law, grandchildren, parents, sisters, relatives, all family members and close friends, thank you.

To coworkers, doctors, authors, song writers, servant leaders, coaches, artists, accountability partners, mentors, professors, counselors, pastors, parishioners, students, strangers, and so many who've helped me learn to pause with Jesus, thank you.

To people who've opened their eyes to read my words and opened their ears to hear my stories, thank you.

To Dianne Chambers, Jim Rovira and others for your editorial work, thank you. To Paul Smith for your editorial help, corrections, and dares, thank you. My brain dances a little differently, so thanks for helping me find the balance.

To Dianne Hall, Doree Rice, Caleb Milligan, and other students, scholars, and friends, thanks for helping years ago with *Beggars Can Be Chosen* and fitting some of those stories into this book.

To college students and epilepsy groups and churches and businesses who enter conversations with me about Jesus and listen to me speak about the Divine Romance, thank you.

To true friends who've helped me survive and endure through so many life seasons, thanks for meals and prayers and conversations.

To Steve Spillman, thanks for believing not only in my writing and our "brand," but in me as a weak man who loves Jesus.

And to my Teacher, thank you. Please continue to help me pause in my hurry to notice Your work, learn more about You, and encounter You personally in everyday life. I am honored to be Your student.

About *Pause with Jesus*

Pause with Jesus, like the other books in the *Pause* series, is designed for both personal and group reading. Each chapter follows a theme, and each theme offers opportunities for individual reflection and group discussion. Readers can calmly reflect on each story, answer the questions, read and meditate on the Scriptures, and seek to apply the theme personally. Small groups also can engage in discussions related to every story. *Pause with Jesus* offers a reminder, a contemplative inspection, and moves us toward action

However you decide to enter a time of reflection and investigation, and whatever your personal situation, begin now. Pause and think. Investigate. By yourself and in the correct group, visit Jesus. Choose to not travel this journey of life alone.

Scholarly material is available elsewhere. Deeper study, more specific spiritual practices, and historical encounters are available elsewhere. Pursue them to add that dimension as you read this book. We all need to study deeply and address crucial questions. Here, though, the words invite us to spend time with *the* Word. That Word, Jesus, is best experienced by practicing various methods of communication through praying, reading, serving, learning, worshipping, confessing, and spending time with true friends. And it becomes more a reality when not limited to such practices, but when those disciplines build such a deep relationship that we are encountering Christ no matter what else we are doing.

Spiritual exercises, questions to consider or discuss, and Scripture conclude each chapter. When practiced alone or among family, friends, and small groups, those exercises can guide each of us in our journeys.

I hope these stories become a part of our stories. Not only the stories of others in history. Our stories. Now.

— Chris Maxwell

> There would never be any greater friend than Jesus. He was the friend who hadn't run from her in fear, the friend who had helped her and healed her. And now Jesus had proven His friendship for all of them in the most beautiful way. —Karen Kingsbury[1]

---

1 Karen Kingsbury, *The Friends of Jesus* (Brentwood, TN: Howard Books, 2015) 141.

Foreword
by Dr. Beverly Oxley

As I read the original manuscripts of Chris Maxwell's latest work, *Pause with Jesus,* I was taken back in my memory archives to March 1997. That was the date I had accepted an invitation of a 4-day pause to hang out with Jesus while attending a spiritual retreat in Atlanta. That "pause" marks a line of demarcation in my life—the Old and New Testaments, the Pre- and the Post, the Before and the After of my life. I now often refer to "before 1997 and after 1997" because the encounter with Jesus was a pause that forever changed who I am.

I chronicled my experience in a journal that I joyfully share with you because, I believe, Jesus wants *you* to experience Him in such a personal, authentic way that will change the course of your *life*. As you **pause with Him**, you make it possible for **Him to pause with you** … and you will be forever changed.

During one of our times of guided prayer, the retreat leader asked us to do a classic exercise of surrender to God—taking time to stop and think about what that means to us personally. He asked us to put our palms down, releasing to God anything that might be keeping us from having a closer relationship with Him. He then encouraged us, when we were ready, to turn our palms up when we were willing to say "yes" to God and "yes" to whatever He has planned for us. As the twelve of us sat in a circle, meditating on our surrender to God, I couldn't turn my hands up! I was struggling with that surrender because of anger and unforgiveness toward my father. Because of the rejection and neglect I had received from my father, I had lived my whole life feeling unloved, unwanted, unacceptable. Long after everyone else had completed the exercise, I finally turned my hands up in surrender. I could never have predicted what happened next.

As I was meditating on what that surrender might mean, I suddenly had a vision of a scene that I will never forget. I was one of the thousands of people on the Mount of Beatitudes on the hillside overlooking Capernaum. (I had been to Israel so I clearly recognized the place.) In this vision I was a child of about five years old, wearing a plain brown dress and sandals, reminiscent of clothing probably worn in Jesus' time. I was there with my mother, grasping her hand tightly out of fear that the throngs of people might separate me from her.

Then, the scene changed to a little further up the hill where I saw a man who was about to begin speaking to the people. He was sitting down but the crowd became quiet when he began to speak and all attention was focused on Him. I recognized Him as Jesus. He was speaking the words that we find in Matthew chapter 5. Suddenly, His eyes riveted toward me and He spoke directly to me: "Blessed are the pure in heart … for they shall see God." I pulled myself behind my mother's dress trying to hide but I continued to look at Him. He stopped talking and just looked at me. His eyes were fixed on me and I couldn't escape His gaze. I also couldn't escape the fact that He was obviously speaking to me.

Slowly, slowly, I walked timidly up the hill to where He was sitting. Our eyes were fastened on each other. When I got close enough, I spoke to Him, "But I am not pure in heart." He continued to look at me with tender, loving eyes. Then, a realization hit me ... "for they shall see God." I KNEW I was looking at God, so it finally began to sink in what He meant ... I was pure in heart. ... I was accepted, not rejected; I was loved, not abandoned; I was invited into relationship, not discarded.

I accepted His invitation by climbing into His out-stretched arms while He held me close to Him and rocked me like a mother rocks her baby. Jesus held me and time stood still. I was transported to a dimension of the spiritual world that I had never experienced before. When I finally left His arms, I was forever changed. I was loved! I was important! I was forgiven! I had seen Jesus!

For almost two months after that experience, I felt a "fullness" in my chest cavity ... a feeling of satiation ... well-being ... contentment. That sensation finally faded over time, but the change in me has never faded. That pause in time with Jesus was life-altering. When we spend time with Jesus, fully immersed in Him, we are never the same. My prayer is that you will take the time to pause with Jesus and let Him take you to a place of no return.

—Beverly J. Oxley, PhD
Licensed Psychologist
Founder and Director, Wellsprings Psychological Resources
Franklin Springs, Georgia

Introduction:
To Enter

I, a citizen of the visible world, know well
the struggle involved in clinging to belief in
another, invisible world. Christmas turns the
tables and hints at the struggle involved when
the Lord of both worlds descends to live by
the rules of one. In Bethlehem, the two worlds
came together, realigned; what Jesus went on to
accomplish on planet earth made it possible for
God someday to resolve all the disharmonies
in both worlds. No wonder a choir of angels
broke out in spontaneous song, disturbing not
only a few shepherds but the entire universe.
—Philip Yancey[2]

Think of reading the biblical stories of Jesus as a written
travelogue. Each verse, story, chapter, account stands alone as
an example of the exquisite life of Christ—as each snapshot
from a vacation individually reflects a unique experience of life.
Unless surveyed as a whole, the completeness escapes and leaves

---

2 Philip Yancey, *Finding God in Unexpected Places* (New York:
Ballantine Publishing Group, 1995) 37.

us grasping mere fragments. The totality of a vacation, missed when viewing individual photos, can be seen by observing the album containing all the pictures, or a video showing the story in motion. Places and people. Good days and bad. Events comprising the entire trip come into focus, accurately portraying a journey that would appear out of balance when only certain pictures were noticed.

This biblical travelogue presents description, like snapshots of a historical person. Knitted together, stories from Christ's life bring into focus a true and astounding picture. More than a portrait of a movement, it is representation of the Man Himself. A Man who loved all the characters of the drama.

The lonely? He loved them.

The misfits? He loved them.

The legalistic, religious, gotta-do-it-our-way-or-we-will-kill-you folks? He loved them.

Demonstrations of that love differ with each scene, but uniqueness merges with unity; the same pure, profound love shines in every sighting.

Who really is that Great Lover? Is He a rigid, lifeless religious man walking under a halo? Is He a lunatic on a neurotic mission to prove supremacy? Is He a moral mercenary determined to demobilize doubters and sinners by running roughshod along a road of political opportunism? Is He a teacher, one of many who have spoken for God through the ages? Or is He, as He claimed, the Incarnation of God?

Turn to a teacher for a definitive argument regarding Christ's deity. Turn to an apologist for an arsenal of proof-texts to ward off skeptics. It's not all here. But as I learn from so many groups that know so much more, I hope they have taught me to learn from Jesus.

What I've offered here is an awareness, a glimpse, of what the Gospel writers were telling us. And what life seems to be revealing. These stories have caused me to see Jesus in fresh ways.

During my childhood I learned to accept the doctrine of Christ's deity. That training has served me well and pointed me, I believe, to the greatest truth in all of life. But, over time, spoon-fed truth can grow stale. Spiritual vision, previously vivid, blurs.

Exploring the narratives again, and with wide eyes, worked. It dusted off death from my belief system. I noticed Jesus in a new way. While watching, I have been shaken. I have been shattered. He laughed and cried. Now, I laugh while typing, as tears fall from my eyes.

I am more aware than ever of both my imperfections and His love for me in spite of my frailty. Watching Him with sinners in Matthew's house, seeing Him gaze at the impish Zacchaeus while certainly grinning, hearing His powerful words stifle the storm: such scenes moved me despite my familiarity with them. Moments of study offered me the impossible task of laying aside my preconceptions long enough to live through the events unfettered by prematurely drawn conclusions. Along the way, I met Jesus. Again. And He is very real, very alive.

And He seems to think we are all important.

It would be far too simplistic to imply that pausing to spend time with Him cures all ills or renders one continually happy. It could be equally untrue and entirely unfair to pretend that uniting our lives with His makes little difference. Deciding to investigate the "who" question of Jesus can start you down the road where the "what," "why," and "how" questions of life become answered in deep, dynamic ways.

If you were, like I was, born and bred in the briar patch of Christianity, thank your parents and your pastors and the martyrs and the saints. But beware. The eternal truths you've come to so readily accept may have grown rusty. Familiarity with theology can make us more religious than real.

Unless Christ invades The Story.

Read and reread the stories about Jesus. Look earnestly for the gentle, strong Leader. Refuse to settle for what you have heard. Do not reject tradition, but do not attempt to confine Christ in a cage of the common. Training may be accurate, but we desperately need the jolt a new look at Jesus can bring.

Annie Dillard, in *The Living*, articulates a caution: "No child on earth was ever meant to be ordinary, and you can see it in them, and they know it, too, but then the times get to them, and they wear out their brains learning what folks expect, and spend their strength trying to rise over those same folks."[3]

---

3 Annie Dillard, *The Living* (New York: HarperCollins Publishers, 1992) 189.

Don't we notice how eager efforts of maturity rob us of childlike earnestness? Our removal of crawling and crying has also robbed our romance. May the thirst for Milk return. May the thrill of Joy refill. May the theory never rob the reformation of faith in Father, Son, and Holy Spirit.

May we refuse to think lightly of Jesus. May we refrain from closeness to Him that merely leaves us callous to His majesty. May we refuse to be ordinary. May we not work so hard to rise above others.

May we pause.

May we pause with Jesus.

In the moments, the adventures, the stories of our lives, may we pause with Jesus.

"Turn your eyes upon Jesus. Look full in His wonderful face.

And the things of earth will grow strangely dim, In the light of His glory and grace."[4]

But you, Bethlehem Ephrathah, though you are small among the clans of Judah, out of you will come for me one who will be ruler over Israel, whose origins are from of old, from ancient times (Micah 5:2).

---

4 Helen H. Lemmel, "Turn Your Eyes Upon Jesus," *Glad Songs* (London: British National Sunday School Union) 1922.

1

The Silence

John 1: 4–5

> Jesus is the one who brings the God I need to
> me. —Eugene H. Peterson[5]

The tilted planet spins by habit in sad silence. Heaven is quiet. No words have fallen from above for four still centuries.

Will earth end this way? Will she slow, sleep, die while her Maker appears absent?

Creator spoke in days past. His voice through creation, His voice through creatures, came clearly. Words thundered, whispered, burned into the conscience of this populated satellite.

The words stopped. People noise continued: words scattered, words sent, words screamed around the earth and up from earth toward the squelched sky. But, from above, nothing.

---

5 Eugene H. Peterson, *Leap Over a Wall: Earthly Spirituality for Everyday Christians* (New York: HarperCollins, 1997) 191.

She flies through skies on course: a planet in place on a pause of maintenance. Can she keep going while weighted with the heavy silence? Will her malaise catch and moor her?

This cannot be all. Creator promised to say more. The Father of worlds vowed to voice His word again.

Tonight, some say, the silence has ceased.

Tonight, some say, the Word has come.

Wrapped in swaddling clothes, lying in a manger, some say, the Word has come.

Sound waves of infant cries: Could it be the voice of God? Shepherds and sheep, mom and dad and angels gather around the center of attention. A Baby born in a world hoping to hear from heaven: Is such a small event worth so much attraction?

God would speak from a mountain or a temple or a television studio. God would speak as a religious leader or a king or a political activist. Not from a barn as a Baby.

The signs shout and dare a world to believe.

Dark doubt has lost a little of its grip on earth tonight, for some reason. The planet of frowns has found a few smiles of wonder tonight, for some reason.

Will a world hear a Word and be healed? Hear a word from an Infant and find faith? Will she?

Time will tell. But tonight the sky is scattered with sound. The music of angels, of stars, of promises fulfilled.

It does appear odd that God would talk this way. And after so long. Yet, if this is God, pray the planet shall listen.

Shall listen, as she spins and flies through noisy skies, shall listen. Pray she shall hear that a long-awaited Word is here.

A Baby cried; the silence died.

The Boy grew: an Alive World sounded louder, filling the vacuum of silent centuries.

A mother, so young, carried Him, held Him. She listened and loved the growing Voice of God.

An old man, bent and crippled for years by bearing the burdens of his fears, deaf and dumb from decades of hearing and saying nothing, heard the Word. His eyes opened; his back straightened. The Word became his friend. The old man learned from his young Tutor. Soon, the man spoke and sounded strangely like his Teacher.

A priest knew the rules and requirements, and met them proudly. He spoke words. Often and in public, he spoke many words. Old words. Dead words. Words added by man, the addendum to a complete, solid-as-stone word given long before. Stories from the Alive Word flew to the ears of that priest who continued reciting his prayers. The priest could not hear God above his own voice.

A lonely woman had heard the words of many men—men who assured her of their love as they assigned her duties. She performed; they paid—that was the love she heard of. But this, this was so new. God's Voice talked to her, talked of giving instead of taking, of choices instead of chores. His words and His tone, His expressions and His explanations sounded like an invitation rather than condemnation. She loved the Word who loved her. She learned the words and lived again, loving a world with them.

A religion collected dust. No sound waves blew across the kept canon. No challenges. No changes. Neat and quiet, the noiseless liturgy disturbed no one. Then, the Word spoke abruptly, shattering the stained-glass cage. Dust flew, but few knew how thick it had grown.

Deep silence dies slowly, if at all.

A place waited. It now felt recreated. The planet danced: an awed world hearing love, finding a Voice of sure celebration.

Joy to the world. To young mothers and bent old men, to lonely women and all who have ears to hear: joy to the world.

The Word is come. Let earth receive His Voice.

READ:

> So Joseph also went up from the town of Nazareth in Galilee to Judea, to Bethlehem the town of David, because he belonged to the house and line of David. He went there to register with Mary, who was pledged to be married to him and was expecting a child. While they were there, the time came for the baby to be born, and

she gave birth to her firstborn, a son. She wrapped him in cloths and placed him in a manger, because there was no room for them in the inn (Luke 2:4–7).

REFLECT:

1. When have you faced and endured times of silence?

2. What did God bring to you?

3. What did you learn?

4. How does Christ's story influence your story?

RECEIVE:

We want. Life leaks. Desires are disappointed. And God, our Father, remains eternally good.
—Jen Pollock Michel[6]

---

6 Jen Pollock Michel, *Teach Us To Want: Longing, Ambition & The Life of Faith* (Downers Grove, IL: InterVarsity Press, 2014) 107.

RESPOND:

- Notice your silence.
- Picture Christ coming to you and being there. Being with you.
- Welcome His presence in the middle of this season of waiting.

2

The Story

Luke 1:30–33

True language has to do with communion, establishing a relationship that makes for life: love and faith and hope, forgiveness and salvation and justice. True language requires both tongue and ear. —Eugene H. Peterson[7]

I am glancing back in time. Into the story. What should we call it? The story of redemption, of transformation, of healing, of hope—according to the beliefs of many about the narrative, those titles fit. For some it's a collection of impossible stories, a mingling of other stories from other times and places, a drama without logic, but a good theory to remind readers to love and care and forgive.

As I read the story of Jesus again, I confess that to me the story really is of healing and hope, of redemption and transformation.

---

7 Eugene H. Peterson, *The Pastor: A Memoir* (San Francisco: Harper One, 2011) 243.

A story about Him and them, about me and us. A story of sacrifice. Summarizing the segments of that story before we glance deeply at a few, I remember my first times hearing the story. From parents, from sisters, from church, from relatives, from teachers, from preachers, from songs, from illustrations, from art. I also remember years reading and studying and writing and teaching about the story.

Now? I want more than *to know about the story*. I want to grasp my tiny role in the larger story. Is that possible? The story indicates so. The story invites a nobody like me into the tale of history and dares me to come. To stay. To live there. Not a brief visit in a service held in one place on one day. A life.

And you? I believe these stories invite you there also.

So what should we do? Enter the storyline. Study the plot, finally detecting ourselves there; spiritually perceiving that story here with us in the now. This now. This moment.

Where do we start? Where the story starts, in the beginning of all. During the voyage of mistake-prone people. Wars and questions and confusion and silence. Jump toward the story's segment of bringing a solution as Gabriel reports the birth of John, a future adventurer and rebel and leader who would work near the water. Read about Jerusalem, about Nazareth, about ancestry of Jesus—that Child to become a world changer, that One related to and promised by the Baptizer, that One these sentences highlight, really.

The Story

An interesting genealogy. History. People. Travelers, natives, doubters, sinners, saints, leaders, followers, rebels: all. Think of the stories within the story. Think about you. Think about me.

An announcement to young Mary. A time together for Mary and Elizabeth. An angel engaged in deep dialogue with Joseph about his sweetheart expecting a child and him knowing this wasn't caused by him. How did they feel? How would we feel? Put yourself in Mary's place. In Joseph's place. Obvious proof declaring the impossible a reality. Trust triggered by an angel's voice. The honor of selection coincides with the humiliation of public opinion. The unlikely happens. The unexpected elected. The normal routine of life interrupted abruptly never ever to be the same.

Let's continue the journey with them. Bethlehem. A decree of Caesar Augustus and the birth of a Messiah as a tiny, needy, fleshly, baby. His skin? His breath? His craving for milk? His eyes slowly, slowly, slowly opening to see a world that would have a very difficult time seeing Him as He was. What did He hear? What can I hear and see and learn about my own cravings, my own eyes slowly, slowly, slowly opening?

Shepherds—those workers in their world coming to see the changer of all worlds. Angels and a baby? Typical guys included in a captivating story.

Magi—at some time in the story coming to visit, amid friction and tension and political insecurity of a leader. A sky and a baby? Mystics and gifts and adventures and governmental power struggles aren't so new after all.

Oh, Jerusalem. Circumcision and a temple. Tradition, rules, guidelines. A place, a nation, a journey. Egypt, Nazareth, Jerusalem: those early years. Yes, a journey. Beginning with travel as preparation for a future journey, maybe. The opinions of others already at work. The realities of a bigger picture also at work.

He grew. He became strong. He was filled with wisdom. Grace was upon Him. Travel and grace, conflict and grace, miles and grace, danger and grace, politics and grace, death and grace.

Does that story allow our names to be included? Can we pause and place grace beside our names?

Very few phrases about Christ's early years. A summary, a scene, some youthful eagerness to make a difference. God as a child? A child: learning to walk and talk and think and grasp realities surrounding Him. Facial expressions? Tone of voice? Eyes? Weather? Noise? Wind? Animals?

People. So many people? What did He know? What did others think, feel, assume as young Jesus walked by? As Jesus visited the temple?

Years of silence on the pages of my Bible. Time traveled on but we aren't given a glimpse. I can imagine. You can imagine. We can imagine. Thinking of our own childhoods, we can imagine. Think of the many meals Christ ate. Think of the weather. Think of His friends. Did His head feel pain from the sun? Did His stomach ache? Were there nights He stayed awake? How did His voice sound as He memorized and sang the songs of King David? How long did Joseph live? What was Mary's facial expression as she glanced outside to see Jesus playing while she knew He wasn't just another little boy?

Suddenly, on our pages of Scripture, Jesus stood up to His mission and walked toward the water. He insisted John baptize Him. Reluctantly, John followed through on his calling and soaked his cousin in the moisture as a reminder of Christ's calling. I imagine the water—its color, its temperature, its welcoming of a Messiah. A dove, a Father, a crowd of observers. What would I have done there? Would I have been interested? Would I have paid attention? What part would you like to play in that drama? Would you want to join in the water? Would you ask Jesus why He was walking away on His own? Would you try to go with Him?

Honestly, I would've expected an adventure toward miracles after drying off the water. Not Jesus. He walked into the wilderness. No food. No friends. Only a battle, a war. His enemy luring with temptations.

Jesus said no to the desires.

I probably would have said yes.

You possibly would have said yes.

Jesus said no.

Then He could begin His adventure in the journey of grace. Selecting disciples. Unexpected, not-very-impressive, not-very-holy, unlikely followers.

You and I might have been selected.

Doesn't that surprise us? Maybe today we can welcome the surprise of His welcome. Observe the face of Christ looking our way. Notice love, not hate; peace, not pressure; kindness, not judgment; invitation, not rejection.

In our hurry of effort and accomplishment, of goals and agenda, of success and completion, let us glance back in time to gain a better view of the now.

Pause.

Visit.

Study.

Realize that maybe this is more than a novel. Accept the reality of this narrative and believe we are in the story.

READ:

> Mary was greatly troubled at his words and wondered what kind of greeting this might be (Luke 1:29).

REFLECT:

1. How do you describe the story of Mary?

2. How do you describe the birth of Jesus?

3. What do you wish you knew about His childhood?

4. What is Christ saying to you about your childhood?

RECEIVE:

> The Christian story, centered as it is on the death and resurrection of Jesus Christ, is the only story for making sense of desire and loss. Not all is right with the world, this world. But our story isn't over. More will be written. —Jen Pollock Michel[8]

RESPOND:

- Revisit this summary of Christ's early years on earth.
- Think of what this means in your situation.
- Celebrate His life in the center of your experience.
- Rest in the reality of His birth.

---

8 Jen Pollock Michel, *Teach Us To Want: Longing, Ambition & The Life of Faith* (Downers Grove, IL: InterVarsity Press, 2014) 105.

3

The Journey

Mark 8:27

How Aslan provided food for them all I
don't know; but somehow or other they
found themselves all sitting down on the
grass to a fine high tea at about eight o'clock.
—C.S. Lewis[9]

The wedding didn't go quite as they had planned. The wine
was missing. For some of us that would be fine, as long as the
right people arrived at the right time and as long as the cake
was there. But they needed more wine and Christ's mother gave
Him a look. You know the look, don't you? Oh, I wish I had
seen it. I can imagine it but I wish I had been standing between
Mary and Jesus, noticing their facial expressions. Jesus resisted

---

9 C.S. Lewis, *The Lion, The Witch and the Wardrobe* (New York:
MacMillian Publishing Company, Inc., 1950) 147.

her lure momentarily. Then He went on about the beginning of His miracle-making ministry by seizing the supply and demand. The participants were pleased.

Mary smiled.

Jesus knew it was time.

The world was about to be changed.

Jesus entered the Passover—did the culture know how ancient promises were becoming realities before them, how the Rescuer was beside them, how the Protector had arrived? So many scenes in this drama. Can't we study them more deeply, grasping depth with personal encounter for ourselves? Can't we read the plot, the context, the story while noticing the magnitude of a word, a conversation, a question? We can. If we do, our full selves dive into the water of an experience. The past visits us here. We discern ourselves amid the ancient mix. The large purpose of the story includes us. Not only for a one time visit to the altar. But for each breath, each thought, each fragment of our own drama.

Let's learn from it all. A mission begins with an unlikely Messiah at thirty years of age. A house of merchandise. An explanation of the story by speaking of how a person is to be born all over again in some way. More baptisms. More travel. A woman at a well—alone and thirsty for not just water.

From Samaria to Galilee, from individuals to groups, from synagogues to homes. A nobleman. A physician. The Sea of Galilee. Peter. Andrew. James. John. Jesus on the go—teaching and inviting and making disciples and casting out hateful spirits and healing ill bodies. What did He do during those days in their lives? What did they learn? What were they desperate for Christ to heal?

From my town to your town. From us to everybody everywhere. From a church auditorium to this room where I am typing. Him. Her. My name. Your name. The name of a friend. The name of that person you or I might hate because of their political views, theological beliefs, or their habits. Jesus still on the go—mentoring and leading and transforming and healing. What do we need Him to do today in our lives? What should we learn? What are we desperate for Christ to heal?

Let us pause and ask. Let us pause and learn. Let us pause and welcome His visit into ourselves as we visit His time so far away so long ago.

Is it difficult to come to Him? When our eyes can't see this King. When our inner selves have been tainted by past perspectives. When doubts about our own importance grow large. Isn't it hard to come to Him? I pray that, even when difficult, we choose to hunt Him. During the chase we might become more aware of this reality: He is the one pursuing us.

Maybe you are Simon's mom. Maybe I'm the leper. Maybe our friend is the paralytic we need to carry Christ's way. Maybe I'm the tax collector. Maybe you are shocked when I am selected to be a part of the same team you've been selected to join. Maybe together we can join in a journey to change the world. Maybe together we see and experience a healing at the pool, a healing in the synagogue on a Sabbath, a welcoming of an unlikely tribe, a welcoming of an unlikely twelve. Maybe together we can hear a sermon on a nearby mountain when blessings come toward the unlikely ones, when we are labeled as salt and light, when explanations of old views offer a fresh glance at kingdom realities.

What if today we hear from Christ? What if the ancient sermon is alive in our minds today? Pick the place. Maybe not a Sermon on the Mount. Possibly a Sermon at the Table. Or a Sermon at the Desk. Or a Sermon on the Plane. Or a Sermon After a Visit with a Counselor. Or a Sermon After a Funeral. Or a Sermon After Losing a Job.

What if we are His audience? What if today is the day for His sermon to us? What if weak people like us are the salt and light of this culture?

I remembered my glance outside last night before going to bed. A game from the NBA finals had ended. The time on my iPhone indicated I was very late for my normal time to climb under the sheets. But I still needed to open the front door and look again. One more time before closing my eyes. A deep breath, a prayer, a chance to notice, a pause.

I did.

A rabbit ran by our sidewalk as I interrupted her expected drama of the night. The wind whispered, not wanting to disrupt but still proving its presence. A dog barked, as it too-often-for-me does. Looking up I saw stars: their beauty, their images, their presence. The sky's darkness moved aside with the light's presence. Staring at a dipper, I prayed, "Creator, please display your love through my life. I can't do it on my own. Light can only crush the darkness if the brilliance is Your love. Shine through me."

READ:

> What good is it for someone to gain the whole world yet forfeit their soul? (Mark 8:36)

REFLECT:

1. What are ways you can live as the salt and light of Christ?

2. If you walk outside tonight before going to sleep, what will you say to God?

3. If you saw Jesus walk up beside you, what do you think He would say to you?

RECEIVE:

When Jesus teaches us to pray by saying, "Your Kingdom come . . . on earth as it is in heaven," he is telling us that the Kingdom of God is continually visiting, interrupting, invading, disrupting, what we *perceive* to be the world. We step into the Jordan River throughout our day. When we let it wash the chatter around us, we hear the voice that says "you are more than your job, your role, your mask. You are mine. And I am pleased." When we step out of the river, we are initiated, illumined, and clean. —Dean Nelson[10]

RESPOND:

Pray this prayer: "Creator, please display your love through my life. I can't do it on my own. Light can only crush the darkness if the brilliance is Your love. Shine through me."

---

10 Dean Nelson, *God Hides in Plain Sight: How to See the Sacred in a Chaotic World* (Grand Rapids, MI: Brazos Press, 2009) 160–161.

4

The Sounds

Matthew 10:39

And all the way, men everywhere were
whispering that the long-awaited Troubadour
had come.

"It is he," they said, "at last he's come. Praise the
Father-Spirit, he has come." —Calvin Miller[11]

My night ended in prayer after I stayed up way too late. I
still woke as early as I always do. And now I am typing words
and imagining scenes. I am reading and writing and thinking:
What did Jesus do? What did Jesus say? How can I pause while
writing about pausing and let these stories be realities in my own
hurried rush toward the next story of my own life?

I glimpse back at the narratives. Each one is so antique and
so distant but so now and so near.

---

11 Calvin Miller, *The Singer* (Downers Grove, IL: InterVarsity
Press, 1975) 119.

He brought the dead back to life. He heard the questions of others and answered with stories. Was He the one guaranteed to come? He didn't look like what they expected and He didn't act the way they estimated, but they wanted to ask anyway. What did it really mean as Jesus told of an easy yoke and a light burden?

See how each part of the large drama is inviting? A woman with the alabaster flask. Mary Magdalene. A request for some sign of proof. Rebukes from Christ to the scribes and Pharisees and hypocrites. He warned His audience; He encouraged His audience. Correction and direction. Confrontation and questions.

And stories. So many stories. Parables to make a point through a narrative.

Just like how this large narrative is pointing our way. Fig trees and seeds and a hidden treasure and a net. All told by a Prophet without honor in His own town. All told by a Lover who cared too much to try to fit in. All told by a Teacher who knew the words would cost Him life.

So, what would He do? How would He respond to the conflict, the tension of this drama? Calms a storm. Tells the truth. Goes home—a place leaders like Him aren't honored. Tells a story about wineskins. Welcomes into His story Jarius's daughter and a woman with an issue of blood.

What moved Jesus? What inspired Him and pushed Him toward action? A law? A regulation? A moment to grab a few more votes in His favor? No. He was moved by compassion. Moved. By compassion.

That compassion caused Jesus to send out His disciples.

See where the story went? See where our stories are now to go?

Before our going out, before our leading others to join us on the journey, let's check ourselves. Are we moved by compassion?

If not, we need to stay here in the story. Jesus did not let His opposition rob Him of compassion. He did not become like those who rejected Him. He proved His love by loving. He proved His character by displaying compassion.

Jesus cared.

For the people, Jesus cared.

He was moved by compassion.

The moving carried Him on in the narrative of conflict. John the Baptizer was beheaded. Five thousand were miraculously fed. Jesus walked on water. Jesus knew some would go away. Multitudes came, more were fed, stories were told, blind could see, Jesus traveled to the land where He would die, Jesus was transfigured, demons were removed, Jesus told of His death.

Tension. A good event and a painful event. A miraculous healing and a promise of death. Blind eyes could see and followers failed to see the realities of His story.

A coin in a fish's mouth. Followers wanting the best seat in the leadership structure. Feast of Tabernacles. Friends and foes. Large numbers and small numbers. Ten lepers and a parable about a Good Samaritan. Time at the home of Mary and Martha. Pausing in the hurry to teach His best friends to pray.

The blind could see. The sheep would hear His voice. Enemies continued plotting. Jesus raised Lazarus from death. A lady, crippled for eighteen years, was healed. Opposition rose because Christ followed love instead of ritual.

Jesus instructed His followers to not pursue the highest seat but to seek the lowest. He coached them to count the cost, told them more stories, revealed the hypocrisy of His religious resistance.

Where do we find ourselves as we pause a moment in this hurried glance at history?

Are we wanting recognition? Are we willing to serve like a Good Samaritan? Are we Mary or Martha or both? Are we seeking to learn how to pray? Are we asking for Christ to bring us back to life? Are we stubborn enough to work through a decade of unanswered prayers and seek a healing right now at this moment? Are we refusing to allow opposition to control us? Are we silently willing to take the back seat?

Jesus continued His adventure of love. A rich man and Lazarus. A coming kingdom. Little children. A rich young ruler and a story of the vineyard.

Where are we in the stories?

I want to ask Jesus if I can sit at His right hand. I want to be close, very close. He loves me and corrects me.

I am a blind Bartimaeus, a short Zacchaeus, a leader not wanting the floor messed up when Mary comes in to interrupt our meeting and pour perfume on Christ's feet.

The Sounds

But I also want to see again. I want Jesus to come over to my house instead of me just climbing a tree to get a glance. I want to take all my oil and pour it all over Jesus.

Today.

Now.

Don't you?

Will you?

As I finish the chapter I hear noise in the distance. Sounds of a parade. Sounds of temple vendors getting their schemes destroyed. Sounds of more stories being told and more questions about those stories. Sounds of a fig tree being cursed. Sounds of promises about future destruction.

Sounds of more stories.

Sounds of more tension and division. Sounds of a Passover. Sounds of the serving of food and the washing of feet. Sounds of betrayal, of desperate prayer, of an arrest, of a trial. Sounds of a Savior being mocked and indicted and betrayed and denied and crucified.

Sounds of silence. Sounds of a surprise.

Sounds of a world about to change.

Let us listen to those sounds. Let us remember.

Let us invite the sounds of those stories into the noise and drama of this moment.

Today.

Now.

Can't we?

Will we?

READ:

> I am sending you out like sheep among wolves. Therefore be as shrewd as snakes and as innocent as doves (Matthew 10:16).

REFLECT:

1. What part of this story thrills you the most?

2. What part disturbs you?

3. What character do you resemble the most?

4. What do you wish Jesus would say to you today?

RECEIVE:

> Imagine you were one of the apostles, traveling around with Jesus, and were given the task of writing his life story. —Keri Wyatt Kent[12]

RESPOND:

- Take time to listen to the sounds of the gospel narratives.
- Imagine the various moods.
- Meditate on the joyful and the sad events.
- End by rejoicing that the large story ends well, and that your story will also move into the world of grace.

---

12 Keri Wyatt Kent, *Deeply Loved: 40 Ways in 40 Days to Experience the Heart of Jesus* (Nashville, TN: Abingdon Press, 2012) 144.

5

The Characters

John 1:39

> When we get a new president in the United States, everyone watches to see who he surrounds himself with—what kind of staff and cabinet he chooses. So the Son of God comes to earth and begins to reveal what kind of 'reign' he will have by putting together his traveling band. —Gayle D. Erwin[13]

Words are interesting creatures. They work together to create stories.

New stories. Life stories. Never-be-the-same stories.

Stories with characters, with setting, with plot, with conflict, with resolution. The stories of Jesus included words guiding readers through each of those segments in the drama of the Word.

---

13 Gayle D. Erwin, *The Jesus Style* (Waco, TX: Word Books, 1983) 19.

Have you visited it lately?

Some of us have read the words so often that we forget the Word as the key character, the designer of setting and plot, the one present in the conflict and the resolution. Pausing and reading it slowly helps me. Pausing and studying it deeply helps me. Pausing and learning from the views of others helps me. Pausing and grasping the large plot helps me. Pausing and visiting each character helps me. Pausing and seeing how my own conflict relates to the tension on the pages helps me.

Maybe it will help you also.

Notice the words revealing the Word.

Start in the first chapter of John's gospel, which includes words about the Word. A Word that was with God. A Word that was God. A Word that made all things, that was all things, that was life and light. John stepped his words aside for a moment, as writers often do. "Light shines," he wrote. "Light shines in the darkness," he wrote. What can darkness do about the light? Nothing. Light wins.

So John's words about the Word, about light, set the scene to reveal a victory already in motion. Before more characters emerge, before more details of the plot are revealed, before conflict and resolution arrive in dramatic elements through many stories, the role of the key character's importance is proven in words.

The Word became flesh.

The Word lived right there near the writer's heart of words.

The author saw that character's glory and concluded that the Word came from the Father, full of grace and full of truth.

The author compared Jesus to His cousin John—a different John than the one being directed by God to craft a written draft of this gospel plot. John the cousin—an unrestrained, discourteous, outdoor preacher wearing basement rejects and living on a diet I personally view as more befitting an animal—became known as John the Baptizer. The reason for that title was his role in baptizing people—placing them in water as a symbolic reminder of how they acknowledged their transgressions and welcomed a spiritual cleansing. John reluctantly baptized Jesus in the Jordan River. God's Spirit revealed to John that his cousin was the Messiah that Israel had anticipated for centuries. What an honor to baptize the man he'd preached about one day arriving. But the thrill of being related to the Savior of the world had a downside; the rise of Christ's ministry would result in the dismantling of John's.

But as another John crafted the words about the Word dismantling a ministry, the story's conflict merges toward an interesting resolution.

No competition. No division. No pick-a-side. No pointing out of hate or insecurity or jealousy.

A pointing of wet hands from the Baptizer to the One baptized, from a prep-work preacher to a called Messiah, from a speaker about God to a Word of God.

John the Baptizer avoided being drawn into a power play. He encouraged his entourage of followers to leave their guild and join with Jesus.

What did they do? What would I do? What would we do?

I would've wanted more questions, more details, more time.

Maybe they had a little more time than the brief narrative includes. But however long it took to occur, the scene reveals they turned from one cousin to another. They left the one telling of a promise so they could follow the Word promised.

Two of John the Baptizer's followers—Andrew and one presumed to be John, the author of this account—followed the Man who the Baptizer called, "The Lamb of God."

They followed the Word—with no detailed words in advance of what type of story they were entering.

They just followed.

How do the words from my personal story relate to their words and their story? How do the words from your personal story relate to their words and their story?

In the beginning was the Word. Words about those days and these days, words about a Word entering their stories and our stories. On a day like today is the Word. Wet from baptism, pointed at by a wild cousin, followed by a few, full of grace and full of truth, He is the Word.

Let us hear. Let us leave behind whatever holds us too tightly. Let us follow.

The Characters

With no detailed words in advance of what type of story we are entering, let us follow.

READ:

> The next day John was there again with two of his disciples. When he saw Jesus passing by, he said, "Look, the Lamb of God!"
>
> When the two disciples heard him say this, they followed Jesus. Turning around, Jesus saw them following and asked, "What do you want?"
>
> They said, "Rabbi" (which means Teacher), "where are you staying?"
>
> "Come," he replied, "and you will see."
>
> So they went and saw where he was staying, and spent that day with him. It was about four in the afternoon.
>
> Andrew, Simon Peter's brother, was one of the two who heard what John had said and who had followed Jesus. The first thing Andrew did was to find his brother Simon and tell him, "We have found the Messiah" (that is, the Christ). And he brought him to Jesus.
>
> Jesus looked at him and said, "You are Simon son of John. You will be called Cephas" (which, when translated, is Peter) (John 1:35–42).

REFLECT:

1. What words do you think about when you read the story of John the Baptizer?

2. What words do you think about when you read the story of his followers leaving and choosing to follow Jesus?

3. Where do you see yourself in this story of words?

4. Where would you like to see yourself?

RECEIVE:

And as I stumblingly try to follow the way Jesus sets out, I realize the good-news truth of God's wisdom and gain a glimpse of what God designed me to do.
—Philip Yancey[14]

---

14 Philip Yancey, *Vanishing Grace: Whatever Happened to the Good News* (Grand Rapids, MI: Zondervan, 2014) 84.

RESPOND:

- Take time to study each of the characters in this chapter's drama.
- John the Baptizer.
- John the author and follower of Christ.
- Jesus the Word.
- Andrew.
- Pause and reflect, seeking to gain a better understanding of yourself and your life with Christ.

6

The Conversations

Matthew 5:1–2

They were filled with questions and they needed answers. They possessed no plan. They simply stood before him on the threshold of hope. —Bill Hull[15]

Why were the two men interested in this leader? What caused them to so willingly accept roles on Christ's inexperienced team?

Probably not the looks of Jesus. Or His voice or His vocabulary or His endorsements. The picture I keep in my office helps my own spiritual formation but the image probably isn't a correct design of Christ. He looks too attractive. He looks too fit for the script. I doubt Jesus was that handsome, naturally baiting men and women with a Hollywood persona. "He had no beauty of majesty to attract us to him, nothing in his appearance

---

15 Bill Hull, *Jesus Christ, Disciple-Maker* (Carol Streams, IL: NavPress, 1984) 18.

that we should desire him" (Isaiah 53:2), wrote the poet/prophet Isaiah seven hundred years before young Mary wrapped the baby Jesus in "cloths and placed him in a manger" (Luke 2:7).

Maybe the witness of John inspired them to take the risk. Maybe their own zeal to find the truth lured them there.

John and Andrew seemed to trust John the Baptizer. They had seen sincerity at the root of his eccentric ways. By following him eagerly, by observing him regularly, they developed an awareness of John's drive to proclaim God's Kingdom. The witness of John the Baptizer gave ample reason for the two to continue their quest toward reality by pursuing Jesus. Like us, they were more ready to accept advice from someone they trusted. They knew John. They knew his passion for right. When he spoke, they listened.

The two men were seeking something, I guess. Aligning themselves with the controversial Baptizer indicated desires for the truth. Questions can guide us toward truth if we let them. If we choose to notice them. If we give ourselves time with them. Doubts and yearnings and dissatisfactions and cravings and rebellion and aspirations are like the hungers we feel when craving a meal. Muscles weaken. Stomach plays percussion. A little dizzy. That starvation, that need, that hope might appear in various ways at different times. But choosing to begin asking the questions that this world seems to have no answers might be the best steps we can take. Even if we stumble a little. Even when we aren't quite sure of destination or time of arrival. Looking, stepping, glancing, wanting, asking, and yearning might help us glance toward grace.

Finding truth really is a grace. But the gift falls into the lap of those who look for it, who long for it, who grasp their inner craving, who follow the urge among the seen toward the authenticity of an unseen kingdom. Sometimes graceful truth seems to stare itself at our unknowing faces—when we least expect it; when we aren't aware of what we're pursuing; when we are just there.

Since a disciple is the one who, by definition, has accepted the role of a pupil, the fact that John and Andrew submitted themselves to learning under John the Baptizer indicated an openness to truth and a willingness to sit at the feet of one believed to possess that truth. From their perspective, following Jesus was the next step in their pursuit.

Jesus noticed their interest. He asked them, "What do you want?" Addressing Him as Teacher, they answered with a question of their own, "Where are you staying?"

Their inquiry sounded like that of a child asking permission to stay up late or like the whimpers of a pet longing to sleep inside sheltered from the cold. "In their awkward way they were asking if they could tag along with him."[16]

Are we seeking to notice life's deep, nagging questions? Do we possess the hunger Andrew and John exemplified? Are we humble enough, courageous enough, wild enough to ask permission to tag along? When asked what we want, are we untamed enough to ask if we can come over for the evening?

---

16 Ibid.

Most of us want to be teachers rather than students. We enjoy thinking we know all the answers, that we see the complete picture. Fortunately, in our story, John's pupils didn't. They hungered for more. They didn't hide the appetite beneath layers of religion or intrigue. They welcomed the status of student. They desired to follow humbly but courageously. They hoped to learn, to grasp, to pursue an often hidden reality—a leader revealing what matters most.

Pausing to study, to learn, to be guided by another—those elements give us chances to develop. Staring as observers doesn't do it. Inviting ourselves over might. Let it begin with an interest. Before another person can significantly impact our lives we must become interested. Then we must let them know of our interest.

I think of myself and wonder if I'm interested enough in what matters most. How deep is my desire? Am I adequately eager? Would I follow John into his unpopular, uncomfortable, not-very-trendy tribe? If not, why not? If not, what life and which leader would I select instead?

If so, would I depart as soon as Jesus appeared? Would I be reluctant? Would John need to be more specific for me? Would Christ need to explain details? Would I be willing to exit if John motioned for me to follow Christ?

I know me well. I like to distinguish the expected outcome. I like details in advance. Advice from a wild leader like John? A nod? A shove? A lure? No proposed results? No promises?

Just a face of grace—would that be enough?

Is that enough today?

"Where are you staying?" asked the seekers. They didn't know the ramifications of that question. Can I ask Jesus that tonight? Can I choose to leave my hurried life of going and doing, and ask where He's staying for the evening? Will I?

READ:

"The one who seeks finds" (Matthew 7:8).

REFLECT:

1. Take time to honestly answer this question people often ask, "Why are you in such a hurry?"

2. Where do you see yourself in the John, Andrew, Jesus conversation?

3. What is Christ inviting you toward right now—though not giving you many details?

RECEIVE:

> You are just a person, after all, in need of help, in need of a friendly place to live. —Vinita Hampton Wright[17]

RESPOND:

- Imagine asking yourself over to spend time with Jesus. Actually, that is what the spiritual disciplines do. The thought is more than a dream. It is a reality.

- Choose today to be with Jesus.

---

17 Vinita Hampton Wright, *The Soul Tells a Story: Engaging Creativity with Spirituality in the Writing Life* (Downers Grove, IL: InterVarsity Press, 2005) 176.

7

The Learning

John 1:34

> It is like a fairy story—the reigning monarch
> adopts waifs and strays to make princes of
> them—but, praise God, it is not a fairy story: it
> is hard and solid fact, founded on the bedrock
> of free and sovereign grace. —J.I. Packer[18]

The new followers of Christ asked a question, "Where are you staying?"

Christ voiced an intriguing answer, "Come and you will see."

Jesus opened His arms, His home, His life to the seekers. "Come"—a central theme of gospel narratives; an essential theme of the Bible; the true purpose of this book—opened entrance into a new world for those two men. The Inviter invited them behind the scenes of history's most remarkable drama.

---

18 J.I. Packer, *Knowing God* (Downers Grove, IL: InterVarsity Press, 1973) 196.

The word "come" is common in the Bible. Before I could hold my research devices on a phone, I could look on paper where my old version of *Strong's Concordance* uses seventeen columns to list the references. In this study's text, the word is a present imperative, indicating a "command to do something in the future which involves continuous or repeated action."[19]

Christ invited them over for lunch.

Think about it. Imagine His voice. Consider your initial feelings, your response.

Come. Come and eat with me. You are welcome here.

And Christ wanted more. He had plans with them for dinner and a nighttime snack. And breakfast. He wanted them to join Him for a meal, for a night, for a future, for life.

If Jesus physically appeared and bid me to sit with Him now, right at this moment, would I accept that intriguing offer? Would I continue reading and writing about Him justifying my approach because spiritual formation includes an awareness of His presence no matter what else we are doing? Would I quote a few lines from Brother Lawrence and work hard to prove I'm "practicing Christ's presence" amid the rushing of my typing and talking?

I hope I would pause. I hope I would come. I hope I would see.

But I know me.

---

19 *Hebrew-Greek Key Study Bible, New Testament,* ed. Spiros Zodhiates (Chattanooga, TN: AMG Publishers, 1984) 435.

It takes work to slow my work. It takes effort to sit, to pause, to come, to see.

Am I the only one? Don't many of us tend to refuse or ignore invitations when the Host is invisible?

Jesus wanted to be with Andrew and John. I think He wants to be with us. Personally with us. Not as a judge grading our performance. Not as an insecure leader forcing an agenda. He longs for humans to fellowship with Him.

Time.

Conversations.

Nothing.

Just being together.

With Him. Alone. Sometimes with Him and them—our friends, His friends, our family, some strangers. Choosing to respond to His invitation. Or choosing to invite ourselves.

Until we do, we might aimlessly float from one attempt at gratification to another, hoping to satisfy a deep longing only Christ can satiate.

It is to such an experience that Christ invited John and Andrew. They came over. And stayed.

Throughout Scripture, biblical writers highlighted that story in a variety of ways. The Gospels speak of "abiding in Christ." The epistles refer to "walking in the Spirit" and to living "in Christ." That latter phrase appears to be the Apostle Paul's favorite; to him, successful individual and community living depended on one's relationship with Jesus.

John and Andrew were invited to Jesus. By Jesus.

Subsequent to the interest of Andrew and John, and the invitation of Jesus, a third act occurred. Jesus immediately began the never-ending task of educating His new companions. He instructed. He was their mentor; He welcomed each as His apprentice.

It can come in many forms under many titles but here's how it happened for them. They joined Jesus at 4:00 p.m. They stayed with Him the remainder of the day. Where does the Bible say He taught them? Where is a list of truths He tried to drill into them?

The Bible mentions nothing about His teaching in this narrative. That is precisely the point. As the invitation comes on the heels of their interest, the instruction begins when they respond to the invitation. As if truth is more caught than taught, Jesus opened His life to His followers.

The degree He offered students could only be earned in active involvement, experiential learning, relational mentoring, life coaching. Isn't that what He is offering us? To come over? To be with? To observe? To learn?

Here, Jesus with His friends, His followers. Jesus with me, with you.

This illustrates the principle of education through personal discipleship. Life's laboratory: the classroom where we pause amid our hurry.

But how are we doing in our responses? Do I receive Christ's invitation to come there? To stay there? In that itinerary of silence and conversations and fishing and waiting and hearing very strange stories, will I invest in the value of time? The call to a life of learning went out from Christ to the initial disciples. He likewise invites us to a life of intimate learning. He longs to be with us.

Responding to His invitation propels the believer into a new existence. Radical changes begin to emerge from the closeness between Teacher and pupil.

The success of educational efforts is proven not just by test scores, but by practical application. Basing our evaluation on that premise, we determine that Christ's beginning efforts succeeded. He didn't quiz the followers or pressure them to do or say something impressive. They responded naturally. Their efforts to influence others with their newfound Truth grew out of their time with the Teacher. Though their time in His classroom had been brief, the impact began an eternal change in their lives.

Jesus had welcomed them. What would they do? Having been influenced by Christ, Andrew, in turn, influenced others. So moved by the One John pointed Him toward, Andrew could not keep the experience to himself. Where would he begin? At home. Bearing the good news, "The Messiah had arrived," Andrew raced to his brother Simon: an arrogant, hard-working fisherman we will learn more about later. Andrew did his part by finding him, telling him, and taking him to Jesus. The Master took it from there.

Where do we fit into this narrative? The story informs me of what I am invited to do. Will I?

Will I be a seeker, expressing desperate interest in the One believed to be the Truth?

Will you?

Listen for, and respond to, His compassionate invitation. Slow from the rush of routine.

Enter the classroom of the Great Instructor. Remain there.

If I live it, if you live it, how many Andrews and Simons will enjoy our influence?

How much will Jesus enjoy us?

How will we be changed?

READ:

> For you have been born again, not of perishable seed, but of imperishable, through the living and enduring word of God (1 Peter 1:23).

REFLECT:

1. How would you describe your recent conversations with Jesus?

2. How have you talked to other people about your relationship with Him?

3. What minimizes your importance in your mind?

4. What is Christ inviting you to do about those thoughts?

RECEIVE:

> We, as sinful, selfish beings, can want freely and yet boldly enter the throne room because of the cross. We can want from God because he—the Holy—has wanted us. —Jen Pollock Michel[20]

RESPOND:

- Think about this story.
- Imagine the voice of Christ.
- Consider your initial feelings.
- Choose now to guide your response.
- Respond by receiving the invitation.

---

20 Jen Pollock Michel, *Teach Us To Want: Longing, Ambition & The Life of Faith* (Downers Grove, IL: InterVarsity Press, 2014) 115.

8

The Found

John 1:51

John kissed the anxious young man and
whispered, "Andrew, it is right: he must
increase, while I must decrease. Go."
—Walter Wangerin, Jr.[21]

Before working on this chapter, I read stories of two
prisoners who escaped a few weeks ago and haven't been located.
Various voices stated their opinions of where the guys are hiding,
if they'll be found, and what should be done so a similar incident
never happens again. And I read a story of a violent attacker
killing nine people—during a church service. A relative of one
victim talked about how she chooses to forgive because she has
been forgiven. Another voice spoke with deep emotional hurt
and said forgiveness isn't an option for such a killer. And many
people keep asking, where was God in all of this? Why didn't He

---

21 Walter Wangerin, Jr., *The Book of God: The Bible as a Novel*
(Grand Rapids, MI: Zondervan Publishing House, 1996) 629.

stop this guy? How can He allow it to happen to people who were spending their time with Him? Will that same God not protect us from the escaped murderers who are still free?

I, of course, don't have answers to those questions or solutions to the problems. What I personally need is to pause and consider Christ. Not just asking about why He didn't do something to keep this from happening. But to ask, can Jesus let me be with Him during this time, during these times, during all times?

Returning to the gospel narratives, I think we glimpse at the answer to that question. Being found by Jesus thrust Phillip into the reality of following the Leader. Following Christ is not a momentary restructuring of our habits and resurrecting damaged hopes. While it does not require complete understanding of all present realities and future ramifications, following Christ is saying *yes*. Saying *yes* while we still have questions. Saying *yes* though carrying doubts. Saying *yes* though holding confusion about killers and people who look down on those of other races and church cliques and self-centered opinions in people very close to us. With all the unknown and uncertain and unclear, we hear or sense or read about a Jesus luring us toward Himself. So we come, with all that we are. We come, to follow Jesus—to observe Him, shadow Him, pursue Him, imitate Him, reflect Him.

By requesting Philip's presence—and our presence—on His mission, Christ offered and offers humans an opportunity to experience life in a new way. "Follow me." Two words as a proposal, an opportunity difficult to turn down. "Come along," invited Jesus, "and be a part of a brand new existence."

Philip's initial act in his new life of following the Inviter reminds us of Andrew racing to find Simon. It was the "first thing Andrew did."[22] Philip, likewise, spread the news. He found Nathanael. He restrained neither his words nor his enthusiasm in attempting to convince Nathanael that Jesus was more than a man. The one who had been found became a finder of others.

I like this news report. A person who found a Leader who cared—true care rather than seeking control from insecurity; true love instead of a selfish ambition for applause.

My mind races back to the killer, still confused by what would propel such hate. My thoughts consider again the hard work of two captives in escape mood, and the desperate search of authorities seeking to locate the men in hiding. My ears are hearing music as I type these sentences—music from the 60s where questions were voiced, feelings were turned into tunes, the common was rejected, hidden topics were exposed. And I think about me—comparing my own heart to each news story, to each song, to the early followers of Christ, to Christ. I ask, Where am I really in this story? Where am I in His story?

I think of a reader like you. Maybe I know your story. Maybe I know nothing about you. Whatever your story, pause to reflect

---

22 John 1:41

on the many stories nearby and this distant story of Christ and His early friends. Don't we need a servant leader like Jesus? Don't we crave a conversation with Him?

For Philip, conversation accentuated his new Leader. He was absorbed by this new way of life. Jesus impressed him. Philip enjoyed the honeymoon emotions of a fresh, untarnished relationship. Such a motivation—while possible and probable—can't fully account for the strength of Philip's pronouncement.

He needed more.

I need more.

We need more.

Men of Philip's caliber tend not to shout "Messiah" simply when fascinated by another person. Philip's initial preoccupation with Christ and his future proximity to Christ stemmed from an awareness of being found. Philip's search for Truth came up empty until Truth found him.

Through that simple, growing conviction came an earnest determination to think about Jesus, to speak of Jesus.

Philip began his proclamation by joining his audience where they were. He went and found Nathaniel where he lived and told him, "Moses wrote of the Messiah. Prophets foretold His coming. Now He's here. It's Jesus of Nazareth, the Son of Joseph."

Nathanael, an Israelite, knew the prophecies of the promised Messiah. By beginning there, Philip left no doubt about his message. He didn't mumble about Jesus being a nice guy. He didn't delay words, depending on Nathanael's response. He stated his case.

Clearly. Correctly.

I'm sure he still didn't understand everything. But he confidently clarified his view: "Jesus is the Messiah."

Nathanael's response sprouted from a seed of prejudice planted within his mind. He had doubted as to whether even a well-meaning person could hail from Nazareth. Certainly not a Messiah. Most of us choose to be less frank than Nathanael.

In that setting Philip responded appropriately. He gave a glimpse of how to counter someone's deeply held judgments. He said, "Come and see."

No, it isn't enough to hear the story.

We are invited to enter the story.

Debates and discussions are needed. There is a time and place for apologetics. Studying and arguing and defending our beliefs are proper when kept in perspective. Nothing, though, compares to saying, "Let me take you to Jesus. You have to see Him for yourself."

Objective faith combines with subjective experience—as in the admonition to "come and see"—to confirm reality. Without a knowledge of the Truth, experience can hardly be trusted. Without an experience with the Truth, facts remain cold and distant. Philip led Nathanael toward both.

Nathanael approached Jesus. Jesus spoke first. His words permitted Nathanael to know that—at least from Christ's vantage point—the two were not strangers. By Jesus, the One he doubted, Nathanael was known. Christ spoke, disarming Nathanael with frankness. Upon learning Jesus' knowledge predated Philip's invitation, his jaw dropped open. His defenses fell. His prejudice crumbled, leaving him in awe. In one sentence he confessed three facets of the diamond of Truth. He labeled Jesus Rabbi, Son of God, King of Israel.

Jesus found Philip who found Nathanael who found Jesus to be who Philip claimed. What a glorious pattern for us to observe and emulate.

In my hurry and my waiting, with my crowds and with my family, nearby and distant, around the autumn leaves and the summer sun, amid the noise and the silence, feeling so much and feeling nothing much at all, when smiling and when angry, when hearing my favorite song and seeing a clear sky at night, among a group of dear friends who accept my weaknesses and alone when I struggle with myself, I want to come and see. Don't you?

To come. To see.

As a lifestyle.

READ:

> The next day Jesus decided to leave for Galilee. Finding Philip, he said to him, "Follow me."

The Found

Philip, like Andrew and Peter, was from the town of Bethsaida. Philip found Nathanael and told him, "We have found the one Moses wrote about in the Law, and about whom the prophets also wrote—Jesus of Nazareth, the son of Joseph."

"Nazareth! Can anything good come from there?" Nathanael asked.

"Come and see," said Philip.

When Jesus saw Nathanael approaching, he said of him, "Here is a true Israelite, in whom there is nothing false."

"How do you know me?" Nathanael asked.

Jesus answered, "I saw you while you were still under the fig tree before Philip called you."

Then Nathanael declared, "Rabbi, you are the Son of God; you are the King of Israel."

Jesus said, "You believe because I told you I saw you under the fig tree. You shall see greater things than that" (John 1:43–50).

REFLECT:

1. Are you being inviting to "come and see" Jesus in a new way?

2. How are you responding to that invitation?

3. What can you learn from Nathanael?

RECEIVE:

> He says just enough to keep us on tiptoe, watching and hoping. —Philip Yancey[23]

RESPOND:

*   Think of Jesus seeing you in some of the places you've recently been.

*   Listen to His words to Nathanael being stated to you personally.

*   Receive those words.

---

23 Philip Yancey, *Finding God in Unexpected Places* (New York: Ballantine Publishing Group, 1995) 240.

9

The Visits

John 2:11

Reading the Gospels, we see that Jesus was often interrupted. But he saw those interruptions as opportunities to love, heal, and embrace people. When you are interrupted, decide that you will see that interruption as one that comes not from the person before you but from God.
—Keri Wyatt Kent[24]

reading the stories again,

i imagine myself

in the scenes—in those moments of

Jesus and His new students

entering the drama of distractions,

---

24 Keri Wyatt Kent, *Deeply Loved: 40 Ways in 40 Days to Experience the Heart of Jesus* (Nashville, TN: Abingdon Press, 2012) 164.

leaving little information for

those of us who desire

the stories within the stories.

He visits people. normal, wounded, weak people.

waiting people. worried people. busy people.

scarred and scared, those people so similar to this one typing words

and those of you reading these words.

let us visit again His method of visiting them, thinking of Him visiting us.

we can go back to His early years.

to visit before the stories of

Jesus in the water and

Jesus battling the temptations,

when very little is written about conversations with Christ's friends and family,

very little is mentioned about what He says—His tone and mood and motives.

when we can guess how much He lived like us and acted like us and felt like us.

and how He was different.

to visit during those stories again and glance inside the scenes,

The Visits

wondering about the face of john after the baptism, the dove, and Christ's departure.

speculating the sound of water, the heat in the weather, the war with a tempter.

counselors ask about hurts from the past. unfulfilled dreams.

painful memories. joyful moments. forgotten realities.

maybe today Jesus is our Counselor,

even though He's the star of the story we're revisiting.

maybe He's enticing us go back to His teens, to His twenties.

tempted like us, He was, in all ways.

imagine the scenes not seen on our biblical pages.

the sound of water.

the push of wind.

the sights through dust, through dark nights, through sand, through trees.

go back to His walk toward a city, toward forming a team, toward us.

shift then into now. deep study combines with a choice to pause—intentionally

revisiting a story, learning the story better, and including the story in

our present lives of hasty, extreme, everything-all-at-once but

missing too much.

i tried

while listening to the braves game

while driving to the atlanta airport late at night for me,

one of the announcers talking about a young pitcher on the mound

who was doing right by not taking this too seriously

but instead was pitching like a kid enjoying the game.

that's what i want to do.

i want to enjoy this experience.

like playing a game, enjoying the gloves and ball and mound.

with respect. with reverence. but like a kid enjoying the disciplines of praying

and reading and noticing the wonder. like a kid staying behind when mary and joseph

and the family left to return home. enjoying conversations with knowledgeable minds

and returning home when confronted by mama.

what is a possible balance of solemn reverence and childlike laughter,

of creative art and simple nothingness,

of deep learning and undemanding contentment,

of pursuing more and enjoying now?

The Visits

seeking to grasp the depths but not forced with hate, i need to
bring Him here.

i need to hear

an inner assurance of the Lover loving me,

the Listener hearing me,

the Savior saving me,

the One baptized soaking me,

the One tempted helping me say no when i crave to do wrong.

through what we call spiritual disciplines,

these actions to engage in dialogue,

these practices to receive a reality our hurried natural selves often
miss,

it happens.

the impossible happens, the interruptions occur,

the dreams come true.

the love occupies us—not just knowing about it but experiencing
it.

let us welcome the

pictures and stories in conversations and songs.

when listening to the news,

when watching a movie,

when stepping away from the normal routine

we go to Him.

or we begin to grasp a reality of Christ coming to us.

bring Him to ourselves? yes, in the now as we

glance back at His birth while we are thinking

of the lights shining and the angels singing

and the audience staring

in all this unexpected reality. in the now as we

gaze at that moment of baptism while our brains listen

to the sound of the water

and imagine the facial expressions and

the Dove

hovering, coming closer,

approving, departing as if with a smile

or an inner applause of satisfaction.

looking back again at the temptation and putting

ourselves there. each personality of ourselves there

staring at our own struggles as we stare

in the city and crave it all as we smell the aroma

of our favorite food or the newest device that we do not need,

as we seek the love and applause and recognition

of a culture addicted to itself.

but He said no, the *no* that comes before the *go,*

resistance before the next adventure.

the visits of friends and foes

remind me of my need of a

visit with Jesus

who finds strange ways to visit me

in my hurried adventure toward another baptism or temptation

to meeting new disciples and noticing a dove,

but now, my visit

is with nothing

but Him.

maybe i'll stay a few days.

READ:

> After this he went down to Capernaum with his mother and brothers and disciples. There they stayed a few days (John 2:12).

REFLECT:

1. What recent life interruptions can you now view as visits from God?

2. How do the stories of Jesus help you grasp Him better in your normal life?

3. How can you become better at pitching like a kid who enjoys the game?

4. What spiritual practices help you choose to visit Jesus?

RECEIVE:

God will find a way to let us know that he is with us *in this place,* wherever we are, however far we think we've run. And maybe that's one reason we worship—to respond to grace. We praise God not to celebrate our own faith but to give thanks for the faith God has in us. To let ourselves look at God, and let God look back at us. And to laugh, and sing, and be delighted because God has called us his own. —Kathleen Norris[25]

---

25 Kathleen Norris, *Amazing Grace: A Vocabulary of Faith* (New York: Riverhead Books, 1998) 151.

RESPOND:

- Take time today to welcome Christ as He visits you in the middle of your busy life.

- Let the stories of His account be methods of visiting with Him.

- Let the beauty around you reveal deep truth about what it really means to be visited by Jesus.

10

The Moments

Psalm 23:1

Prayer is a way of language practiced in the
presence of God in which we become more
than ourselves while remaining ourselves.
—Eugene H. Peterson[26]

"Is this easy for you, Chris? As I hear you talk, it sounds
simple. It even sounds fun. But thinking of me making myself
do this stuff feels impossible."

I appreciated his honesty during dinner at our spiritual
formation conference. Those sitting beside us were nodding
while listening to the conversation.

I admitted the journey is fun but also confessed it isn't
always simple. I asked him to tell me more.

---

26 Eugene H. Peterson, *Tell It Slant: A Conversation on the
Language of Jesus in His Stories and Prayers* (Grand Rapids, MI:
Wm. B. Eerdmans Publishing Co., 2008) 267.

"Most of us here this weekend want to pray more. We want to know God better. I've studied the spiritual disciplines and tried really hard to do what I've studied. But I start and stop. I never keep it going."

A lady beside us agreed. "Thanks for giving us a better view about prayer. I just struggle to believe I can do this like you are doing it."

I asked for examples of how they've tried to pray, and what often stands between them and Jesus. The second part of that question caused another guy to stop eating and offer his admission. "What do I let get in the way of my prayer life?" he asked. "Just about everything. Like her, I start but don't keep it going. My mind goes in other directions. I start feeling guilty and when I'm guilty I don't feel worthy to talk to God. So, like I do in many areas of life, I become busy. That busyness you talked about this morning has become my new addiction. I get busy and see results. Prayer, I am sorry to say, doesn't seem to bring me many results."

He then looked the other way as he ate the food he'd held on his fork while he talked. His friends—my new friends—nodded. The man who began our dinner discussion agreed: "I think we all want this. But do we want it enough?"

Their honesty opened doors of their own awareness of themselves. When guilty feelings lure us toward silence we often leave situations alone. Conversations like our retreat's dinner confessions initiate a process of becoming more conscious of tendencies, addictions, expectations, limited information, and incorrect assumptions. I asked their permission to join me that evening as we opened the session on "Lead us in Prayer." In that evening session I had hoped to move from the lessons about spiritual formation to applications. From what to how. From educational to experiential. We decided to initiate the gathering with their questions and confessions. I knew the audience would relate.

Can't we all relate to their thoughts? Haven't we all battled the tendencies to be lured away from prayer and into actions we can feel, actions we seem to control, actions that appear to provide results clearly and quickly?

The conversation was perfect for our evening's introduction. The crowd's faces were nodding. A few raised hands and spoke similar feelings in their own words.

After the confessions, the tension was clear. The conflict was obvious. We want time with God, but do we want it as much as we want other things? We want time with Jesus but how do we spend time with an invisible Messiah? We want time with the Spirit but is praying and reading the Bible really making any difference? Is it making us any different?

Before suggesting some *how to* steps, I merged from the conversation with my new friends to a teaching about how our chats with Christ might not be that different from our talk at the table.

A chat. A conversation. Including various methods of dialogue—requests, confessions, appreciation, silence, questions, research—is how we can view prayer.

I quoted Adele Calhoun, from one of the many books that I suggested the audience read: "Spiritual practices don't give us 'spiritual brownie points' or help us 'work the system' for a passing grade from God. They simply put us in a place where we can begin to notice God and respond to his word to us."[27]

I repeated again my phrase about how we need to see these conversations with Christ as a divine romance rather than a list of religious duties. I said, "The practices of studying, singing, reading, listening, silence, meditating, intercession, petition, fasting, resting, giving, serving, and many others are all various ways of continuing a conversation with Christ and developing our relationship with Him." I told stories of time with those we love, and how that ride from a doctor's office with a son, that flight to another country with a spouse, that dinner at a nice restaurant with a friend you haven't seen in five years, that look from a child's eyes after they finally returned home, and that early morning walk through the sand hearing the ocean's waves wash in all contained different moods, different intentions, different words, different feelings, different outcomes. But the common outcome from such moments can be the development of relationships.

Think about yourself and the time you spend with people you love the most. Think about yourself and the time you spend doing what you personally love the most. And now think of

---

27 Adele Ahlberg Calhoun, *Spiritual Disciplines Handbook: Practices That Transform Us* (Downers Grove, IL: InterVarsity Press, 2005) 19.

where Jesus fits in. Don't condemn yourself because you aren't making enough room for Him. This thought process is to help you learn ways to invest more time with Him. Ask yourself, "If I enjoy eating lasagna at that Italian restaurant, don't I sometimes find a way to eat there?" Most of us do.

I know when my one favorite TV show begins its new season. I know when my favorite sports teams play. I respond when hearing my favorite song. I dive in the water when I am ready to swim. Why? I have chosen to make time, to learn, to enjoy those encounters.

Spiritually, we develop stronger relationships with the Jesus of this book by choosing to do what this book is about: pausing. We pause to notice the stories we are reading on these pages. We pause to ask Him to do things we want to see done—we label it prayer and we can practice in many different ways, but we make a choice to take action and to enter conversation with a God we do not see with our natural eyes. We pause to slow our hurried pace a little to notice creation, a friend, a stranger, a person from a different nationality, a song, a word, a deep wound needing healing, a profound joy needing to be expressed, a victory needing to be celebrated, a terrible decision needing to be confessed to a trusted friend. We pause to study Scripture—a full epistle, a particular context, an often misused quotation, an intriguing verb. We pause to listen to a song we often sing without fully grasping the depth of the words frequently resonating from our voices. We pause to cry. We pause to laugh. We pause mentally and emotionally with a deep breath when a day's hurried schedule won't slow for even a moment.

We listen to a sermon. We visit a dying friend and ask for healing. We visit a sad friend and ask for hope. We drive a long distance alone realizing we aren't alone. We choose to give up a meal to spend that time focusing more on our Loving God than we would have if our routine had remained the same. A wide array of possible methods of experiencing Christ.

We see with faith, with imagination, with beliefs. We act through those beliefs by engaging in conversation with that Invisible Presence: listening to what our normal ears might miss but our spirits might grasp, requesting something from the One who has invited us to ask, thanking Him for the many wonders we frequently forget, journaling our honest thoughts as a way of releasing our burdens to the Leader who offers to carry those heavy hurts for us.

That is prayer. That is spiritual formation.

God moments. Your way of communicating to Him won't be exactly like mine.

No, this isn't always easy for Chris. No, it won't always be easy for you. Yes, I have to schedule and plan times where I practice the disciplines—otherwise I'll never apply them. Yes, those practices guide me toward my desired outcome—an awareness of the God-with-me-life no matter what else I am doing or what time of day it is.

Scheduled times with Jesus make unexpected awareness of Jesus more likely. At least for me.

Even if "this stuff seems impossible," begin. Enter the conversation. Invest time.

Prioritize the moments with your True Love, apply various methods of conversation, and see where the story goes.

READ:

> I call out to the Lord, and he answers me from his holy mountain. I like down and sleep; I wake again, because the Lord sustains me (Psalm 3:4–5).

REFLECT:

1. What questions would you have asked if you were in that conversation at dinner?

2. What steps should you now take to apply this explanation of spiritual formation?

3. When do you plan to begin?

RECEIVE:

> Mastery of every discipline is not the goal. Surrendering to God is. —Adele Ahlberg Calhoun[28]

RESPOND:

- Set five simple goals of your own spiritual development.
- Refuse to let fears or failures control you.
- Enter the conversation with Christ.

---

28 Adele Ahlberg Calhoun, *Spiritual Disciplines Handbook: Practices That Transform Us* (Downers Grove, IL InterVarsity Press, 2005) 21.

11

The Invitations

Matthew 4:17

What will you create? Who will you help? What connection will you make? What will you dare to care about? There are so many opportunities, so many chances to find beauty or to ease suffering, that the easiest thing to do is to pretend that they don't exist. Because if they *do* exist, if that little girl will live a better life because you showed up, if that void will be filled because you cared enough to do something about it . . . if we actually recognize the opportunity that's in front of us, what are we to do about it? We'd have no choice but to change things for the better, to take our turn and make a difference. —Seth Godin[29]

---

29 Seth Godin, *What to Do When It's Your Turn: and It's Always Your Turn* (CITY, ST: The Domino Project, 2014) 87.

Applying the disciples as methods of communicating with Christ helps us get to know Him better. Revisiting the biblical stories helps me grasp what this truly means. So, let's return to the conversations and experiences Jesus had with His followers.

Let's continue the journey back in time to observe Christ's invitations, traveling in reverse to the shores of the Sea of Galilee. No media blitz or highlight hits. Only Jesus and a few fishermen. The sight? The smell? A little different from modern stage productions. The stink set the scene for reality. It was another day in the life of normal people. And another day in the Life of Jesus.

The fishermen, Simon and Andrew, "were not decrepit men with gray beards and bent backs so often depicted in paintings. . . . Rather, these were rough, tough young men at the powerful peak of early manhood, either in their late teens or early twenties."[30] Andrew came to Christ through the witness of John the Baptizer. He then introduced Simon to Jesus. Then they returned to their work as "partners with James and John in Zebedee's fishing business."[31] Jesus saw them fishing. He voiced His invitation: "Come, follow me and I will make you fishers of men."

Once again Jesus swung open the door by speaking the word, "come." To the young fishermen, Jesus said, "Come."

---

30 W. Philip Keller, *Rabboni* (Fleming H. Revell, 1977) 84.
31 Ibid., 17.

Inviting them to approach Him, to be with Him. Think about it. Did He ask them, "Will you come?" Did He tone it as an exclamation: "Come!"?

Jesus had seen them before, remember? At the first meeting, Andrew asked Jesus where He was staying and Jesus answered, "Come and see." Jesus showed personal attention. He spoke specifically rather than voicing a general welcome cloaked in religious jargon. Andrew was a person to Christ, not a pawn in the game of amassing a substantial following.

A person.

A person like me.

A person like you.

Andrew stayed with Jesus for the remainder of that day. He came away so impressed that he told Simon he had found the Messiah. Jesus didn't ask them why they had returned to fishing. He merely invited them. "Come," He said. "Be with me." A simple, concise invitation.

Jesus then expanded the invitation by qualifying the welcome. He encouraged them to not only come but to follow Him. A journey toward Christ develops into a life of following Him. Noticing isn't enough. Observing isn't enough. As mentioned earlier, "to follow" means to come after, to become an adherent, to pattern one's steps after. "Come hear me preach, then go back as you came" wasn't the strategy. By saying, "Come, follow me," Jesus implied, "Come and be a part of what I'm doing in the earth; let's experience life together."

And they did it. They left their nets at once and followed Him.

The word translated "left" was used elsewhere to speak of dismissing a wife for the purpose of divorce. It was also used to mean forgiving sins completely. So they divorced their nets and followed Jesus. In doing so, those two young brothers left what was possibly the only occupation they had ever considered.

They turned their backs. On their income. On their security. Why? To follow a Man who traveled from town to town telling stories.

Doesn't sound very intelligent, does it?

But does it sound like what we all crave?

James and John climbed out of their boats and onto the path of Jesus. "Immediately" they left their nets and their father. Inherent in this biblical concept of following was the reality of leaving behind. Saying hello to a pause with Jesus often says goodbye to a busy action.

Or maybe it means thinking about His love while not very convinced about it ourselves.

Or maybe it means slowing down a little, welcoming deep beliefs and fresh smiles and good food and nice music on a day like today.

Or maybe it means saying goodbye to whatever addiction or pleasure or preference stands between us and the Fisherman.

Jesus vowed to give new life to those who gave their existing lives to Him. Why come and follow? Is there a valid reason here? To the followers, Christ pledged to rearrange their lives. He guaranteed to transform fishermen into men fishers.

He sees us as people, not as numbers.

We are individuals in His eyes. We have potential. He believes in what He can do with us.

Peter and Andrew returned again to fishing at some point after that encounter. Luke records, in chapter five of his account, that Jesus approached them and directed them to a fishing jackpot. There the Savior altered His phrasing to reemphasize His purpose for their lives: "Don't be afraid. From now on you will catch men."[32]

And they traveled on with Jesus. The world was never the same. We are here in the present reflecting on this story because of the roles those followers played in the original narrative.

But isn't Christ's invitation just as real and personal to us today as it was when Jesus welcomed His disciples by the water? Isn't He inviting us to Himself, to His adventure, to His mission, to His story? Isn't He meeting us in our daily lives as we fish, as we write, as we read, as we hurry?

---

32 Luke 5:10b

READ:

As Jesus was walking beside the Sea of Galilee, he saw two brothers, Simon called Peter and his brother Andrew. They were casting a net into the lake, for they were fishermen. "Come, follow me," Jesus said, "and I will make you fishers of men." At once they left their nets and followed him.

Going on from there, he saw two other brothers, James son of Zebedee and his brother John. They were in a boat with their father Zebedee, preparing their nets. Jesus called them, and immediately they left the boat and their father and followed him.

Jesus went throughout Galilee, teaching in their synagogues, preaching the good news of the kingdom, and healing every disease and sickness among the people. News about him spread all over Syria, and people brought to him all who were ill with various diseases, those suffering severe pain, the demon-possessed, those having seizures, and the paralyzed; and he healed them (Matthew 4:18–24).

REFLECT:

1. Would you be surprised if Christ met you in your everyday routine and invited you to follow Him? Why?

2. What would keep you from following Jesus?

RECEIVE:

> If you let the real Jesus into your life, the God whose supreme desire is your happiness and fulfillment, you will want to throw out anything that is going to stop you from reaching His Kingdom. —Brennan Manning[33]

RESPOND:

- Welcome the teaching and preaching of Jesus.
- Welcome the healing of Jesus.
- Let the news of His stories spread through your thoughts, your conversations, your decisions.
- Hear His words: "Come and follow me."

---

33 Brennan Manning, *The Relentless Tenderness of Jesus* (New York: Revell, 2004) 11.

12

The Storm

Psalm 23:2–3

He didn't doze off the bow where the spray would get him and the whitecaps slapped harder. He climbed back into the stern instead. There was a pillow under his head. Maybe somebody put it there for him. Maybe they didn't think to put it there till after he'd gone to sleep, and then somebody lifted his head a little off the hard deck and slipped it under.

He must have gone out like a light because Mark says the storm didn't wake him, not even when the waves got so high they started washing in over the sides. They let him sleep on until finally they were so scared they couldn't stand it any longer and woke him up.

—Frederick Buechner[34]

34 Frederick Buechner, *Peculiar Treasures* (New York: Harper & Row, 1979) 63.

This story begins with Christ's invitation to His followers: "Let's go over to the other side of the lake." Maybe the words had warmth. That's my guess. How do you think the disciples felt as He directed their next steps? They had seen miracles. They had heard Him claim to be God. So now? He invited them to take a boat ride.

Invitations make us feel wanted, particularly when they come from one we admire. Knowing our presence is requested gives us cause for thinking that maybe we aren't as terrible or as unloved as our self-talk says.

What could have been a wonderful time of fellowship began turning sour from the start. The trip's Organizer fell asleep as they embarked. Exhausted from the endless stream of needy people, He hardly waited for all to board before finding a pillow and sailing into sleep.

The picture of Christ asleep on a pillow reveals His human side. We can relate to being worn out. Tired. In need of a break. We know about that, don't we? As I read this story over and over, I thought of the many times I had read it in the past, the times I have talked about it and written about it. I once journaled a poetic confession of my own thoughts—we will read that in our next chapter.

For now, let's remember the beautiful scene, where there does appear to be something wrong. The sight would be more fitting if the boat had drifted peacefully through calm, clear waters.

But a storm arose. Such weather hazards were common.

Jesus sleeping at a time like this seems rude. Lives were at stake and Jesus was on a momentary vacation. How could He sleep?

Let's focus on an important truth. Despite the fact that Jesus slept, He was still there with them. The first way Christ wants to touch us in our place of fear is with His presence. We may immediately want His hand of deliverance. What we need most and what He never fails to bring is this: Himself. His hands at work are wonderful. But we need His face nearby more than His efforts, His achievements, His accomplishments.

What is your present storm? How are you being affected by it?

Storms have a way of making us afraid. We might deny our fears; we might pretend all is well; we might work hard in the middle of the thunder. But hidden fears can still control us. Our decisions. Our relationships. Our plans.

In the story, Christ's disciples felt they were in great danger.

They were.

Jesus was sleeping through the tempest! I'll be honest; I can see why His followers didn't let his nap continue. They woke Him in desperation. He might be at peace while we are all suffering in angry waves, but I want Him to wake up and help us.

I believe God does work miracles.

He may be quiet, His presence unseen. Our prayers may seem directed to a Father who habitually sleeps. But He's not asleep. He is with us.

Can we ask for anything more wonderful? By gracing us with His presence, Jesus gives the greatest gift of all. Even when other people offer us companionship instead of cliché-ridden comments, our lives find enrichment.

But still, I would've wanted quick action. Not the slow calming of the storm. I want the storms stopped immediately.

They aren't stopped, though, are they?

The financial storm! The relational storm! The health storm! The business storm! The addiction storm!

Sometimes Jesus seems awake and at work, quickly bringing a solution.

Other times? He seems to be asleep.

And that is what He is helping me learn more about. A rest amid a storm. A nap while winds roar. A moment of calmness while everything around is anything but calm.

I am trying to learn that. I am trying to live that.

It's not easy.

But it is healthy.

His presence adds an interesting aspect to our perception of a dilemma. When we realize that we aren't alone, we can choose to begin viewing situations the way He does. We normally look at frightening and frustrating detours of life through lenses tinted by hopelessness. Unlimited by time, space, and elements, Christ sees situations differently. The disciples failed to realize what Jesus knew, that being with Him in the place He wanted them was the safest place on earth. Jesus knew it. The teasing of the storm could not cloud His perspective. Obtaining God's perspective releases us from this assumption: for all to be well things must turn out the way we feel will be best.

What can help us rest even when busy, even when awake, even when facing a storm? *Pausing with Jesus* in a life of prayer, meditation, worship, fellowship, Bible study, and ministry moves us toward obtaining proper perspective. Talking to and listening to God in silence? That helps. Reading Scripture and reaching out in service? Those help. We become transformed when we view our storms through the lens of hours studying the struggles of Apostle Paul, of days helping an elderly friend pay bills and purchase groceries, of nights of staring at starry skies and acknowledging God's handiwork, and of mornings humbly engaged in private prayer.

Maybe you know the rest of this story. Jesus calmed the storm. He also rebuked the disciples for their lack of faith. He protested their inclination to not let His presence affect their perspective. A change in perspective might have made the storm seem less threatening and made the boat feel safer. After all, wasn't Christ still there with them?

I am trying to hear what He is saying to me now in my storms. I am wanting you to hear what He is saying to you in your storms. What if we change? What if even when the situations stay stormy, we remain calm?

I want that to be me. I want that to be you.

Admit it, though. Often we need more.

And often, as in this story, Jesus stands to His feet and dramatically tampers with evidence. In their storm He shouted at the forces of nature. He commanded them to relinquish their destructive behavior. He loudly informed the violent disturbance that the time for a pause had come.

I love the wording of the text: "the storm subsided, and all was calm."

I think about this story every time my family rides on a boat with my sister's family. The water, the noise, the waves, the calmness. I have taken a nap on their boat.

Today, whatever the weather and how strong the waves, maybe Jesus can help us pause and rest. And today, if the storm has gone on long enough, maybe Jesus can pause the surroundings and declare that the time for a calming miracle is now.

READ:

> One day Jesus said to his disciples, "Let's go over to the other side of the lake." So they got into a boat and set out. As they sailed, he fell asleep. A squall came down on the lake, so that the boat was being swamped, and they were in great danger.
>
> The disciples went and woke him, saying, "Master, Master, we're going to drown!"
>
> He got up and rebuked the wind and the raging waters; the storm subsided, and all was calm.

"Where is your faith?" he asked his disciples.

In fear and amazement they asked one another, "Who is this? He commands even the winds and the water, and they obey him" (Luke 8:22–25).

REFLECT:

1. What are the worst storms of your life?

2. Where was Jesus during that season?

3. How are you learning to rest during a storm?

4. How are you learning to believe in a miracle?

RECEIVE:

Then in spite of the wild pitching, he stood up on the back thwart and spread his arms and cried out louder than the winds, louder than the crashing seas: "Peace!"

His body seemed small below the lightning and the violent night. Nevertheless, his voice was the thunder itself: "Peace!" he commanded. "Be still."

And the boat sighed and settled into smooth water. The sleeves of the torn sail dropped straight down on Simon's shoulders. No one spoke. A universal calm covered everything, so that it was the disciples' ears roaring, unaccustomed to quietude. Little waves slapped the hull. Simon, gaping and blowing sprays of water, whispered, "Who is this? What kind of man *is* this?" —Walter Wangerin, Jr.[35]

RESPOND:

- Pray two prayers today.
- Ask God to end the present storm you are experiencing.
- Ask God to help you rest peacefully until He does.

---

35 Walter Wangerin, Jr., *The Book of God,* 676–677.

13

The Sometimes

Psalm 23:4–6

True fellowship with others will only achieve
its God-given richness when it is rooted in our
practice of silence and solitude with God.
—Bob Kilpatrick and Joel Kilpatrick[36]

sometimes

the noise of silence

and the closeness

of distance

remind me of how

painful love really is.

wanting and wishing

---

36 Bob Kilpatrick and Joel Kilpatrick, *The Art of Being You: How to Live as God's Masterpiece* (Grand Rapids, MI: Zondervan, 2010) 86.

while doubting and waiting,

we question our worth and our value.

i know i do.

and i doubt i'm alone

in the endeavor of aloneness

in the middle of a crowd

and sadness

inside the mask of so

happy and so glad and

so sure.

walking with numb feet.

dancing to no music.

waiting for a hidden kiss.

and waiting more for more and more and more.

or something else.

anything else.

am i wanted? loved?

important? of value?

i've been told so.

sometimes i think so.

but other times,

The Sometimes

like now,

the noisy silence

of aloneness

shouts a sound of nothing

at all.

far away can be

as close as possible.

silence can contain

a volume of fear.

a smile can be only a

mask to cover the wounds

from that love so painful.

so powerful, so pleasurable, so promising,

and, yes,

so throbbing.

but what if it's worth it?

that love,

what if it's worth the contraptions that seem so unlike love?

what if the sadness of

a death, a departure, a defeat

is actually okay,

somehow in the

larger craft of life?

in the tension of noble and excruciating,

delightful and miserable,

what if that pressure, that tension,

can in some way

lead to a deeper healing?

staring at the mirror, i notice hurt.

standing beside a friend, i observe wounds.

glaring toward the many, i detect internal injuries.

listening to a morning's melody of hurry, i discern angst.

those convoluted, throbbing, bleeding hurts

hurt deeply,

even when hidden by coverings of religious smiles

and impressive performances,

veiled by tedious chores

and scholarly debates,

disguised by busy days and busy lives,

of life

and death

and nothing, really.

The Sometimes

just covered, in denial of reality

sometimes.

the camouflaged lives aren't really life

until that time of something,

some thing,

some change,

some choice,

some shift,

some confession,

some shaking into reality

of releasing decades of sorrow.

like a confession toward a lover who actually hears all

and still loves in the end.

like a prayer toward a listener who risks all

to bring restoration.

like silence with a companion who is okay

with no words and no smile and no thrill and no high.

time by the river, listening to the movement.

time at the ocean, feeling the waves changing shifts so suddenly.

time on the mountain, as near to the top as possible and seeming

so distant from any highest peak.

time alone and being okay with that; enjoying, not escaping.

time with a crowd and being healthy with that; experiencing, not comparing.

time of nothing

at all

now.

no longer a fugitive, now a person.

no longer a victim, now a champion.

no longer a performer, now an artist

slowing designing

while being designed

in this sometimes joyful,

sometimes crazy

adventure of life.

maybe not a david defeating a goliath,

but david the poet, singing to a hidden dad.

maybe not walking on the water

or calming a storm,

but napping in the boat, uncontrolled

by any tempest anymore.

sometimes,

i guess,

that is best.

a nap, unhurried,

while being healed.

READ:

> My heart is not proud, LORD, my eyes are not haughty;
> I do not concern myself with great matters or things
> to wonderful for me. But I have calmed and quieted
> myself, I am like a weaned child with its mother; like a
> weaned child I am content (Psalm 131:1–2).

REFLECT:

1. What parts of this poem remind you of your own
   thoughts?

2. What assumptions lure you away from rest?

3. What steps should you take to schedule time for a nap?

4. Are you willing to take those steps and make this a reality?

RECEIVE:

> Jesus seemed to know that seeking simplicity—particularly in regard to food, clothing and appearance—is a journey. He comforts us by saying that God knows we need all these things and that they will be given to us as we seek God and the kingdom.
> —Jan Johnson[37]

RESPOND:

- Schedule an appointment with "rest."
- Choose to breathe slowly—let each time you inhale and exhale be a peaceful moment of receiving and releasing.
- Close your eyes.
- Hand your worries over to your Heavenly Father.
- Rest.

---

37 Jan Johnson, *Abundant Simplicity: Discovering the Unhurried Rhythms of Grace* (Downers Grove, IL: InterVarsity Press, 2011) 154–155.

14

The Looking

Luke 4:36–37

In the morning Jesus' disciples discovered that he had not returned all night long. He was not in Simon's house. They went out and looked for him, but found him nowhere in the city.
—Walter Wangerin, Jr.[38]

Bibles fill many shelves. Some are grabbed, opened, studied, investigated, prayed, preached, learned from. Some are kept in particular places, expecting to never be opened or moved or touched. Some serve as items of history. Some provide daily nourishment for those who want to learn and live better after reading those pages. For many, pages aren't turned as often these days since we carry devices with various versions and commentaries and personal note Bibles with us in the same gadget that sends notes, makes calls, and offers global confessions of our latest endeavors.

---

38 Walter Wangerin, Jr., *The Book of God,* 653.

As we pause with Jesus, we invited you to enter the stories. Looking into history we might notice more about truth. Looking into biblical stories we might notice similar conflict and questions and needs and transformation that we encounter in our deep selves.

We might tend to ignore uncomfortable texts. By doing so, we are refusing to really look and see what is there. We are resisting the reality that Christ might be looking at us through the stories.

Let's pause and walk slowly through one of the narratives. In Luke chapter 4, we read a story that invites us to pause. To be. To notice. To study and think and process. And to do all of that with Jesus on our minds and in our hearts.

The story begins with Jesus leaving the synagogue and going to the home of Simon.

To pause appropriately and visit the story, we need to grasp the context. One of the negatives about including verses for us to read and pray and memorize in each chapter is that we have only included the particular verses. Much more knowledge can be obtained as we read and study the bigger picture—verses before and after, the larger context of the book the passage is from, the historical context of the original audience, and the even larger context of entire Scripture—before rushing a quick conclusion about how it relates to us in the present.

If I spoke about life with epilepsy and mentioned the need to drink more water and get more sleep, a few phrases could be quoted, misunderstood, and taken out of context—similar to how many news reports work these days. My long talk about better health could be quoted correctly but revealed incorrectly: "Drinking and sleeping can help each of us." The sentences before and after describe the water we should drink and the best way to sleep; without those previous comments, the one sentence could indicate heavy drinking of something other than water that might lead to more sleep after all.

Similarly, we need to study and meditate on Scripture by grasping the context as well as possible.

In the stories of Jesus, this book visits them to emphasize a particular theme—personally aware of Christ in everyday moments of life. In studying the various gospel narratives to gain a deeper understanding, we should read how other writers learn from the stories and supply information to help us learn more from the stories. In every account, we should read the before and after—again, valuing the context. In Luke's narrative of this study, we should read the before and after.

So, remembering all of that, let's go back to Jesus and the synagogue and Simon's house.

The context for our reading is Luke 4, and it begins with Christ's temptation. Read it. Slowly and deeply. Listen to the words. Visit the conflict as you want to know and experience the verses we are highlighting in this chapter.

Next, listen as Jesus teaches in synagogues with power—hear the applause, see the crowds drawn to Him, meditate on the words Christ stated and the texts He quoted, and mentally stare at the faces of the audience when their minds drastically changed. His exciting declaration ended with rejection.

Pause with Jesus for a moment right there. Fulfilling His life mission included a crowd seeking to throw Him off a cliff.

How did He respond? By traveling on and continuing to do His purpose. He taught the people. A rejection in one place did not control His words in the next place. He drove out an evil spirit from a man, and then talked more—amazing the audience.

Next? He left the amazed audience. Jesus seemed to do that often. In the middle of ministry momentum, He paused and left the large stage. He entered the home where Simon's mother-in-law was suffering from a high fever—as Luke the Doctor described it.

The people made a good decision: they asked Jesus to help her. Studying this story and mentally seeing what Christ does can change us deeply. If we allow it.

Jesus bent over her.

Jesus rebuked the fever.

Jesus left her.

She was healed, got up, and began waiting on the crowd. Honestly, Luke needs some editorial assistance here. Shouldn't he have taken this story deeper? Shouldn't he offer a framework, a model of how this type of healing would always work if we did just what Jesus did? Shouldn't the doctor tell us that not everyone will always be healed just the way she was healed?

Well, maybe Jesus wants us to pause in the moment, in the story, in the narrative, and notice the drama's movement.

The Looking

The day was ending. More people came to Jesus. More were healed. More evil spirits came. More were rebuked.

Then comes the part of the story that seems to fit best in the context of this book. A new day comes. Jesus had left to find a solitary place. He didn't keep the drama going. He left. He went out. He chose to pause.

Though His adventure of solitude didn't last long, let's not delete it from the story. Yes, the crowds found Him and begged Him to stay. Yes, Jesus moved on to more cities and more people and more chapters in His story of redemption.

We can go to Luke 5 and read of Christ calling His disciples, healing more people, eating with sinners, and answering a few questions.

For now, though, maybe we can stay in the story of Christ healing many. Maybe I can become one of the many. Maybe you can become another one.

Our fevers are probably very different from Simon's mother-in-law's fever.

But the Jesus who bent over her is the Jesus who can bend over us, or look calmly at us, or place oil on us, or invite us to dinner, or remove the hurt in us, or help us get up to wait on the many people who might be coming over to hear Him again, to see Him again, to know Him again or for the first time.

As the sun sets again and as the sun rises again, maybe we are the ones who choose to bend over into a solitary place with our Healer.

READ:

> Jesus left the synagogue and went to the home of Simon. Now Simon's mother-in-law was suffering from a high fever, and they asked Jesus to help her. So he bent over her and rebuked the fever, and it left her. She got up at once and began to wait on them. At sunset, the people brought to Jesus all who had various kinds of sickness, and laying his hands on each one, he healed them. Moreover, demons came out of many people, shouting, "You are the Son of God!" But he rebuked them and would not allow them to speak, because they knew he was the Messiah. At daybreak, Jesus went out to a solitary place. The people were looking for him and when they came to where he was, they tried to keep him from leaving them. But he said, "I must proclaim the good news of the kingdom of God to the other towns also, because that is why I was sent." And he kept on preaching in the synagogues of Judea (Luke 4:38–44).

REFLECT:

1. Are you willing to be looking into Christ's stories in new ways?

2. Are you willing to see how Christ might be looking at you?

3. How can you look at crowds and love them better?

4. How can you look away from crowds and be healed today?

RECEIVE:

What meetings are scheduled? What tasks must be accomplished? Which people do you have to interact with? Invite Jesus to be with you in those encounters and chores. —Keri Wyatt Kent[39]

RESPOND:

- Find practical ways to balance your life better.
- Plan times with people.
- Plan times away from the crowds.
- Let Jesus direct you in showing His love to all people even in those unplanned moments when you are looking more like Him than you ever believed you would.

---

39 Keri Wyatt Kent, *Deeply Loved*, 26.

15

The Distractions

Psalm 46:10

When Jesus visits his friends Mary and Martha, in Luke 10, Martha is caught up in preparing a big meal and fumes at her sister, Mary, for hanging out with Jesus rather than helping her. When she asks Jesus to intervene, he must shock her when he rebukes her for worrying over the details of dinner rather than following her sister's example. —Amy Simpson[40]

I'm trying to be Mary. Trying hard. Too hard.

Isn't that the point?

Maybe there are more points and more lessons I should learn but I know this: I see myself in Mary and in Martha.

I am distracted and obsessed and busy and occupied and at work on all the preparations that must be made.

---

40 Amy Simpson, *Anxious: Choosing Faith in a World of Worry* (Downers Grove, IL: InterVarsity Press, 2014) 93.

I notice the needs, the *so many* needs, nearby and far away, in friends, in family members, in strangers. Apparent needs. And hidden needs.

But do I need to be needed in an attempt to help their needs? How can I know? If I'm hurrying to the gate and anxious to board the next flight to the next place is that my kitchen?

No, I'm not just like Martha. I can't cook. I can't fix anything in a house or vehicle or computer. But do I think I can continue my duties of doing and doing all on my own strength while hoping He's watching?

Couldn't my Martha personality become a better person if my Mary desires were followed more?

That lure to pause. That moment to take a slow, deep breath, to inhale, to exhale, to inhale again slowly, to exhale again slowly. That meal of tasting and chewing and swallowing slowly, completely, refusing to rush the moments by. That conversation of deep listening, true eye contact, and sincere care.

Maybe my *Martha work* on a presentation or in a meeting, my *Martha work* of words to type or words to speak, my *Martha work* of time with the hurting, would all be more alive if I sat beside Mary and Jesus. If I listened. If I stayed. If I waited. If I refused to have something to prove or do or finish or achieve.

I love Mary. I love Martha.

I need them both.

But like them both, I need Jesus.

We need them both.

The Distractions

But like them both, we need Jesus.

Maybe during our Martha moments we can invite Jesus into the kitchen. Ask what music He wants us to play because surely He knows the meals are cooked better when music is on. Would we sing along with Jesus while asking Him what He wants for dinner?

Remember this. It was Martha who opened the door for Jesus. We often treat Martha like she told Jesus to stay outside while she spent a few days fixing the house to impress Him. She welcomed Jesus.

That is good.

That is what I need to do.

But she was "distracted by all the preparations that had to be made." That, though understandable and common, wasn't good. That is what I often do. Don't you?

Let's try this. Pause a moment and contemplate on the story. Each scene: distracted. . . by all the preparations. . . that had to be made.

Distracted? By her perfectionistic side? By her humble heart? By the need to impress? By sincere courtesy? How many preparations? Did they all really need to be made?

Add that sentence to your story. What are your distractions? What are you preparing for? Do they really have to be made?

As I contemplate on her story, their story, and my story, I think of my doing. I know the importance of many actions I take. I investigate the motives in my impure self. I am aware of my distractions. I reach conclusions like this: I need the heart of a Mary while using the hands of a Martha. And this: be still. And this: sit a while. And this: rest. And this: invite Jesus to the kitchen.

Instead of asking Jesus to tell someone to come help me, what if I need to go to Him in this moment?

"Martha, Martha," the Lord answered, "you are worried and upset about many things, but few things are needed—or indeed only one. Mary has chosen what is better, and it will not be taken away from her."[41]

Needed? Few things. Really, only one.

I pray I choose the better, like Mary. I pray it will not be taken from me.

Even when the kitchen is calling.

Even when the flight number is announced and I am to board the plane. Even when my name is called and I am to stand on a stage. Even when my name isn't called and my value feels questionable. Even when doubts and fears suggest I avoid their existence by working so hard I hardly know what's really inside me and beside me. Even when my fingers type these words on this keyboard to appear on this screen and later on this book's pages, I am to be with Jesus.

Seeing. Hearing. Being. While busy, while sleeping, while hurting, while laughing. In the crowd or just us. When I feel like He is there and when I feel nothing at all.

---

41 Luke 10:41–42

When my Martha-self is in a hurry, I pray to stay and be.

With Jesus.

Now.

READ:

> As Jesus and his disciples were on their way, he came
> to a village where a woman named Martha opened
> her home to him. She had a sister called Mary, who
> sat at the Lord's feet listening to what he said. But
> Martha was distracted by all the preparations that had
> to be made. She came to him and asked, "Lord, don't
> you care that my sister has left me to do the work by
> myself? Tell her to help me!" "Martha, Martha," the
> Lord answered, "you are worried and upset about many
> things, but few things are needed—or indeed only one.
> Mary has chosen what is better, and it will not be taken
> away from her" (Luke 10:38–42).

REFLECT:

1. How do Martha's actions resemble you?

2. How do Mary's actions resemble you?

3. Add yourself to this story. What would you say? What would Jesus say to you?

4. How would you respond?

RECEIVE:

What good, then, is it to pursue a calling if the pursuit may destroy you? How do we balance this tension between the ceaseless call of work and life itself?
—Jeff Goins[42]

RESPOND:

*   After adding yourself to this story, as suggested in REFLECT, now add this story to your own circumstances.

*   Think of how you can learn to work like Martha and pause like Mary.

*   Write a list of specific ways to live that balanced life.

---

42 Jeff Goins, *The Art of Work: A Proven Plan to Discovering What You Were Meant to Do* (Nashville, TN: Thomas Nelson Publishing, 2015) 185.

16

The Enticement

Matthew 10:7

> I suspect Matthew also understood what it felt like to don the leathery, emotional hide worn by the desperately down-and-out who need no reminder that good people consider them undesirable. . . .They would seek help among the righteous, but nicely dressed church people appear sanctimoniously superior and profess a religion that merely promises to exchange one burden for another. —Charles R. Swindoll[43]

Each of our stories is different. Our moods, our feelings, our beliefs, our motives, our records of many poor decisions: when we meet Jesus or when Jesus meets us, each story is unique. It's also that way when we read the biblical stories of those Jesus invited to pause.

---

43 Charles R. Swindoll, *Jesus: The Greatest Life of All* (Nashville, TN: Thomas Nelson, 2008) 89.

Peter, Andrew, James, and John received their call while hoping to haul in a decent meal. Matthew sat, running his business, when Jesus entered the stage.

Matthew was a tax collector—not the expected vocation of one whose life was about to change forever because of encountering Christ. He worked his job as many in his field did in those days. Probably not always honest, not always trustworthy, not always holy.

Again, as we continually see occurring, Jesus entered Matthew's world. It hurt the reputation of Jesus—if we want to call it a reputation—among the churchy folk. But the Matthews of this world are like the Matthew of this story. They are, we are, real people who make poor decisions and live our lives desperate for love.

Jesus does that. He loves.

He displayed that love to Matthew.

Matthew never forgot it either. Later, when he listed his own name in the rundown of disciples, he identified himself as a tax collector (Matthew 10:3). Other Gospel writers edited it out, maybe wanting "to forget that an apostle was engaged in his despised work, but Matthew himself never ceased to wonder that a social outcast such as himself should have been selected by Jesus for this high office."[44]

---

44 R.V.G. Tasker, *Tyndale New Testament Commentaries: The Gospel According to St. Matthew* (Grand Rapids, MI: Wm B. Eerdmans, 1961) 106.

The Enticement

Jesus was a terrible politician. He never played his cards right. By approaching Matthew, Jesus raised the eyebrows of denominational executives. By speaking to Matthew, He gave them ammunition to use against Him. Then Jesus caused their ulcers to flare up when He invited Matthew to come along.

He continued blowing His chance at religious and political stardom. He went home with Matthew and ate with him, sitting among the undesirables. Instead of working His way to the top of the religious establishment, instead of rubbing shoulders with the right people, Jesus palled with the wrong people. He entered the homes of the hated and saw them as important.

What went through Matthew's mind? We can only speculate. So, let's do. He surely had to wonder why he jumped so suddenly from his way of life to follow a controversial Teacher. Was there something in the person of Jesus that drew Matthew? Christ did not resort to persuasive gimmicks; He only presented Himself as the drawing card for New Life.

Over the years we have missed the awesomeness of the Savior's call. Let's notice it now. It is simple, but life-changing. It is straightforward, but loving. The invitation creates more questions than answers. Matthew's abruptness shocks us. It indicates that we often miss something in our response to Jesus. Notice how Frederick Buechner describes it:

> Where will our following take us, for instance?
> God only knows where it will take us, and we
> can be sure only that it will not take us where

we want to go necessarily but where we are
wanted, until, by a kind of alchemy, where we
are wanted becomes where we want to go.[45]

By pausing from his moment and following Christ, Matthew
changed. We now open a book with his name in it—a book
telling the story of the Word by using words remembered from
scenes and experiences so real that Matthew couldn't help but
tell all who might read.

How can I learn from him and his story? How can I hear
again today—as I type at this table, as I think at this table, as I
hurry at this table, as I seek to accomplish at this table, as I desire
to prove to myself that maybe I'm okay after all at this table—
the Voice staring at me with loving strength and compassionate
power as He says, Come?

Maybe as we walk outside together and I leave behind my
addictions and my religion, He might start telling me stories I so
desperately need to hear:

> The Kingdom of heaven is like a treasure
> hidden in a field. When a man found it, he hid
> it again, and then in his joy went and sold all
> he had and bought that field.

---

45 Frederick Buechner, *The Magnificent Defeat* (San Francisco: Harper & Row, 1966) 99.

> Again, the Kingdom of heaven is like a merchant looking for fine pearls. When he found one of great value, he went away and sold everything he had and bought it (Matthew 13:31–33).

Will we remain at our own tables or follow Him?

Matthew rose from his tables of habit and security. He received the Kingdom.

The Pharisees sat glued to their tables. They might have been originally sincere, but that had evolved into self-serving religion. They rejected the Kingdom.

"Get up from your table," Messiah still says. "Come to mine. At my table I offer bread and wine as proof of my eternal Friendship. At my table I have a place for you. Won't you come?"

Jesus wants to enter your home.

He sees you as important.

READ:

> As Jesus went on from there, he saw a man named Matthew sitting at the tax collector's booth. "Follow me," he told him, and Matthew got up and followed him.

> While Jesus was having dinner at Matthew's house, many tax collectors and sinners came and ate with him

and his disciples. When the Pharisees saw this, they asked his disciples, "Why does your teacher eat with tax collectors and sinners?"

On hearing this, Jesus said, "It is not the healthy who need a doctor, but the sick. But go and learn what this means: 'I desire mercy, not sacrifice.' For I have not come to call the righteous, but sinners." (Matthew 9:9–13)

REFLECT:

1. What is the table where you are presently sitting in your life journey?

2. How do you feel as you think of Jesus coming to you and looking your way?

3. How do you feel as He invites you to come His way?

4. Do you respond to His invitation?

RECEIVE:

> In Christianity God is the great and merciful Initiator. He reaches down to needy humanity. In all other religions of the world humans reach up in search of reality and salvation. The "but God" rings through apostolic preaching. God broke through and entered history: He loved the world; He acted in the interests of the world; He sent His Son to procure salvation.
> —George W. Peters[46]

RESPOND:

- Pause.

- Think about your table of comfort and security.

- Think about Jesus looking your way and inviting you to come with Him—out the door and toward a new adventure of grace.

- Physically stand and walk outside as a reminder of your spiritual adventure.

---

46 George W. Peters, *A Theology of Church Growth* (Grand Rapids, MI: Zondervan Publishing House, 1981) 97.

17

The Gentle

Matthew 11:28–30

He invites us to accept Him as our teacher so that we might learn how He coped, how He managed stress, how He faced the pressures of the world with tact and grace, how He forgave, how He ministered to others, and how He remained connected to the Father.
—Charles R. Swindoll[47]

Experts instruct us that a leader must be self-assertive, confident, demanding and direct. Though Jesus exhibited many characteristics we would consider compatible with today's leadership models, He surprises us with the two traits listed on His résumé. He said He was gentle and humble. How drastically different from qualities expected of contemporary leaders.

Gentleness and humility seem out of character for a king, especially the King of an eternal kingdom. Such qualities score

---

47 Charles R. Swindoll, *Jesus: The Greatest Life of All,* 89.

few points on the modern management meter. We look for the driven leaders, even if their driving takes them over the backs of others. If they are determined to make it to the top, we want them on our team.

Jesus said, "I am gentle. I am humble." The contrast from our assumed traits of leaders is striking.

His résumé informs potential buyers that He's considerate, unassuming, and meek. That He's humble—choosing to take the low road, refusing to promote self. The same word speaks of mountains and hills made low.

Our identity comes from One who described Himself with those two words: gentle, humble.

Jesus elaborated further on Himself and promised that His yoke is easy, His burden is light.

An easy yoke? It fits. It is appropriate. It is not forced. It is practical.

A light burden? Not much weight to it. Not holding us back. Not controlling us.

That is so much what we need in our days of stress and conflict. To stop a moment and consider this option—beside the covered external realities of duties forcing us; beside the compelling inner voices equaling our worth and value to our accomplishments—offers peace, hope, healing. We might not be able to stop today's schedule, but we can choose to enter a new perspective toward what we are carrying.

So that is our leader, Jesus. He described Himself as a gentle, humble man who has for His followers a properly fitting yoke and an easy to carry burden.

After revealing His qualifications as the inviter, Jesus told who He welcomes. The invitation reads: "to the weary and burdened."

Whoever is tired and exhausted. Whoever has a schedule too full that there's no time for self-care. Whoever continues going and going and going and going with no end in sight. Whoever has pursued that dream they thought was promised to them but never arrived. Whoever kept their own part of a promise but was lied to on the other side. Whoever can't sleep at night. Whoever can't stop eating. Whoever is afraid to eat at all because of the weight that might come with it. Whoever stares at their stats of success and thinks, *Is this all there is?* Whoever hopes no one ever really gets to know them.

Charles Swindoll sums up the condition of the weary ones:

> Lots of things are fine in themselves, but our strength has its limits. . . and before long fatigue cuts our feet out from beneath us. The longer the weariness lingers, the more we face the danger of that weary condition clutching our inner man by the throat and strangling our hope, our motivation, our spark, our optimism, our encouragement.[48]

48 Charles Swindoll, *Growing Strong in the Seasons of Life* (Portland, OR: Multnomah Press, 1983) 136.

The traditional wording of this verse, "those who labor and are heavy laden" (Matthew 11:28, KJV), paints an accurate picture of Christ's intent. The invitation goes out to those who labor in the service of formal religion, those who labor to satisfy or justify themselves, those who feel like they must always prove something, those who must reach that next goal, those who push and shove and drive and demand, those who are doing too much for many wrong reasons. There are many types of labor that place us in the position to be qualified for this invitation.

Think of your life and your labors.

In what ways are you burdened? Religious activity? Damaging habits? Self-hate? Depression? Guilt? Fear? Loneliness? Dependence? Confusion? Isolation? Denial? Refusal to seek help? Refusal to face reality? Refusal to accept forgiveness? Choosing very little self-care? Allowing emotions to control decisions? Abuse you received many years ago? Abuse you are still receiving? Church wounds? Pornography? Substance abuse? Side-effects of medications? Finances? Politics? Giving up? The future? Negativity? Harshness? Disorganization?

Add your own weights to the list. Add your burdens, your responses to your burdens, your method of adding new burdens to deal with burdens you've held a long time.

Whatever the source of weariness for you, please realize an invitation has been spoken by the gentle and humble Savior. He can alleviate the crushing load of guilt. He can calm the storm of fear. He can free us from the prison of habit.

In this long journey of life, we are people desperate for someone to do just that.

I'll not, however, make it sound like a quick, easy, emotional high. No, it is better than that. It is taking what we are reading here, pursuing Christ in a new way, and receiving this as reality. It is a journey—a process of choosing to become better aware of ourselves, of choosing to know we are people in need of help, of choosing to obtain help from Jesus by spending time with Him rather than attempting performances for Him.

Let His first three words become our life words: Come to Me. Come, He invites us. To Him, He invites us.

In all of today's commotion, hear Him near you. Imagine a gentle, caring, loving facial expression. Envision a smile—a true smile. See His eyes looking directly at you—not controlling but caring, not judging but inviting.

Inviting us.

Inviting us now.

READ:

> Come to me, all you who are weary and burdened, and I will give you rest. Take my yoke upon you and learn from me, for I am gentle and humble in heart, and you will find rest for your souls. For my yoke is easy and my burden is light. (Matthew 11:28–30)

REFLECT:

1. What are the reasons you are so weary and burdened?

2. Can you think of any practical steps you can take to alleviate some of those reasons?

3. What does it mean to you that Jesus is gentle and humble in heart?

4. How can you practically take these words from Christ into your life?

RECEIVE:

"Take my yoke," Jesus said, which in effect means, "Connect with me for learning and training purposes.

Imitate me in all that you do. I will be next to you, the wiser, stronger, seasoned one who will impart to you all that I am." —John W. Frye[49]

RESPOND:

- Write a list of the burdens you've been carrying too long.

- Release what you can externally.

- Prayerfully surrender to Christ internally any of those remaining weights.

- Receive His gentle love and healing today.

---

49 John W. Frye, *Jesus the Pastor: Leading Others in the Character & Power of Christ* (Grand Rapids, MI: Zondervan Publishing House, 2000) 76.

18

The Thirst

Luke 15:1

> We know that we desire happiness, purpose and love. Yet the simplest desires seem to be beyond our reach. Is there anyone who has identified what blocks us from what we seek but cannot find? —Rebecca Manley Pippert[50]

"All to Jesus I surrender; all to Him I freely give. I surrender all. I surrender all."

I listened to the song last night. I stopped singing along and started listening to the lyrics. After the music ended and the voices were silent, my mind continued hitting replay. Over and over and over. All. All to Jesus. I surrender. All. All to Him. I freely give. Do I and will I ever trust Him? In His presence daily

---

50 Rebecca Manley Pippert, *Hope Has Its Reasons* (San Francisco: Harper & Row, 1989) 16.

live? The lyrics have lived through time and seasons and styles and stories. The lyrics wanted to live again deep inside me. The song invited me to pause with Jesus.

I experienced that at a conference where I spoke to families with special needs. Often, the one speaking is actually the one needing to receive what the speaker says. I needed my own words. I needed the reality of my own story. I needed a glance into the larger story of us all together in that room, and all people in every room, surrendering all. And as a friend played the keyboard and sang that ancient song, words were breathing and dancing and daring me to hear again, believe again, receive again, surrender all again.

The service concluded and I thought, "How many times do I fail to pause and receive a song's true meaning?" I felt like a deep thirst had been quenched. The end of a service was a new beginning for me as I became better aware of my own thirst and the source providing for me—as I surrendered myself and admitted my need for water. His water.

Jesus knows about the need for a drink. Once, when alone and worn from His journey, Christ sat by a well. His robe flashed no religious logo. A woman approached to draw water.

The middle of the day was a strange time for her to undertake this task. People habitually took care of such business before the sun became their enemy. Gathering in the morning or evening hours made the climate work in their favor, as labor turned into an arena for conversation. They socialized as they worked.

Not that woman. She came during the heat of the day, revealing her standing with society. Enduring the relentless afternoon sun was better than suffering the silence of a condemning group gathered around a well.

Jesus did not look away when she arrived. He was traveling a path religious experts knew not to travel. Devout Jews despised the people of Samaria. Jesus didn't. He refused to allow man's religious rules to hinder His purpose. Travel through that city? Converse with a woman? A Samaritan woman? A Samaritan woman known for her wicked ways? Such acts were never done. Except by Jesus. Social tradition did not control Him—He touched all those ignored by the religious rule-keepers.

All.

To.

Jesus.

The clean hands of strict legalists wouldn't applaud His efforts. But He continued. And He reminded listeners of His purpose: "It is not the healthy who need a doctor, but the sick. I have not come to call the righteous, but sinners to repentance." (Luke 5:31)

Jesus remained on course despite strong winds of pharisaical opposition that judged Him guilty by association. Their muttering confirmed that He remained true to His agenda: "This man welcomes sinners and eats with them." (Luke 15:2)

Christ embraced people others avoided.

Jesus.

To.

All.

Jesus allowed the woman to approach and He initiated conversation. Thirsty beside a well, He asked the woman for water.

Jesus also perceived that the Samaritan woman was thirsty for more than a drink of water. Her shifts from man to man indicated a craving for acceptance that eluded surface relationships. Jesus did not preach. He probed.

How often are we thirsty for Jesus, but seek to drink—or perform or work or control or demand or deny—elsewhere? How many of our friends are thirsty for the Living Water the woman at the well encountered?

Read and study more of this story. Don't stop there though. Think about the words about surrendering all, surrendering all to Jesus. Think about how He might be waiting for you—right now, today, no matter what we have done or where we are living or what have historically done to crave our thirsts—as you walk in for a drink.

Engage in the conversation.

Surrender all.

Receive a sip.

Never go back to the former life.

READ:

> Now he had to go through Samaria. So he came to a town in Samaria called Sychar, near the plot of ground Jacob had given to his son Joseph. Jacob's well was there, and Jesus, tired as he was from the journey, sat down by the well. It was about the sixth hour.
>
> When a Samaritan woman came to draw water, Jesus said to her, "Will you give me a drink?" (His disciples had gone into the town to buy food.)
>
> The Samaritan woman said to him, "You are a Jew and I am a Samaritan woman. How can you ask me for a drink?" (For Jews do not associate with Samaritans.)
>
> Jesus answered her, "If you knew the gift of God and who it is that asks you for a drink, you would have asked him and he would have given you living water."
>
> "Sir," the woman said, "you have nothing to draw with and the well is deep. Where can you get this living water? Are you greater than our father Jacob, who gave us the well and drank from it himself, as did also his sons and his flocks and herds?"
>
> Jesus answered, "Everyone who drinks this water will be thirsty again, but whoever drinks the water I give

him will never thirst. Indeed, the water I give him will become in him a spring of water welling up to eternal life."

The woman said to him, "Sir, give me this water so that I won't get thirsty and have to keep coming here to draw water."

He told her, "Go, call your husband and come back." "I have no husband," she replied.

Jesus said to her, "You are right when you say you have no husband. The fact is, you have had five husbands, and the man you now have is not your husband. What you have just said is quite true."

"Sir," the woman said, "I can see that you are a prophet. Our fathers worshiped on this mountain, but you Jews claim that the place where we must worship is in Jerusalem."

Jesus declared, "Believe me, woman, a time is coming when you will worship the Father neither on this mountain nor in Jerusalem. You Samaritans worship what you do not know; we worship what we do know, for salvation is from the Jews. Yet a time is coming and has now come when the true worshipers will worship the Father in spirit and truth, for they are the kind of worshipers the Father seeks. God is spirit, and his worshipers must worship in spirit and in truth."

The woman said, "I know that Messiah" (called Christ) "is coming. When he comes, he will explain everything to us."

Then Jesus declared, "I who speak to you am he."

(John 4:4–26)

REFLECT:

1. How do we often pursue filling our thirsts incorrectly?

2. How can those methods bring more harm?

3. What poor decisions have you made that Jesus can forgive?

4. How do you respond to His instruction to go and sin no more?

RECEIVE:

> Admit you were wrong. Apologize to anyone you weren't empathetic to. Own it so that you can start working on it. —Jon Acuff[51]

RESPOND:

- Take time to read and study this story of Jesus and the lady.

- Think about her past decisions, her reputation, and her thirst.

- Notice how Christ invites her to Himself.

- Hear Him saying those same words to you.

---

51 Jon Acuff, *Do Over: Rescue Monday, Reinvent Your Work, and Never Get Stuck* (New York: Portfolio/Penguin, 2015) 190.

19

The Walk

John 6:20

In any case—pray no matter what. Praying is rowing, and sometimes it is like rowing in the dark—you won't feel that you are making any progress at all. Yet you are, and when the winds rise again, and they surely will, you will sail again before them. —Timothy Keller[52]

What next?

Five thousand men, plus women and children. That's how many they fed with five loaves of bread and two fish. So, what next? How could Jesus match that? Once again, Jesus shocked observers with His follow-up maneuver. No press conference. No announcement of date and time and location of His next major miracle.

---

52 Timothy Keller, *Prayer: Experiencing Awe and Intimacy with God* (New York: Dutton, 2014) 260.

In what appears to be the height of missed opportunity, Jesus left. He just left. He sent away the crowd and made the disciples take a boat out on the lake. He went into the hills to pray.

What a drastic change of pace. From crowds and miracles to solitude and silence.

Then another swift shift. The silence didn't last long. Howling wind and crashing waves pierced the stillness of Christ's time alone. The disciples, having sailed about four miles, found themselves in the middle of a lake with howling wind and crashing waves. But without Jesus.

Or maybe not. Maybe He wasn't as distant as He seemed. Maybe He was with them—though not as close as they would prefer—during their storm.

Jesus had spent most of the night in prayer and appeared to the disciples between three and six in the morning. His means of arrival? Jesus walked on the water to them. They panicked, but Jesus said, "Take courage! It is I. Don't be afraid." (Matthew 14:27b)

No matter how deep the water or how strong the storm, it helps to remember the Savior remains close. In His time He speaks. Looking for Him and listening for Him reminds riders we aren't alone.

Peter acted impulsively as usual. "Lord," he said. "If it's really You, tell me to come to You on the water." Peter the Risk-Taker assumed that if Jesus could exert enough upward force to offset gravity's attraction and remain afloat amid rapid water, He could do the same for Peter.

> We hear a great deal about Peter's walk of
> faith when, taking his eye off the Lord and
> looking at the waves, he began to sink; but we
> do not hear much about the strong faith which
> enabled him to leave the boat, and take even a
> few steps on the water to Jesus.[53]

I admit—I'm shocked by his willingness. I'm typing these words between my teaching times at a camp for people with special needs and their caregivers. A few of the experiences here intend to challenge us up a tree or in a boat or on a horse or in silence or in stillness or in rest or encountering life together. Some of us are limited by clear weaknesses. All of us are hindered by some weaknesses.

But, in some way, Jesus might want us to take a few steps, to take a small risk, to take a chance, to take the tiny faith we say we have and soak it into action.

Thinking of my own struggles while writing this story, I commend Peter's boldness. We can't fully know his motive, but let's not write him off too quickly as just a loud mouth continually diving into the sea of attention. Maybe he wanted to prove himself; but then, many of our motives are a little contaminated.

---

53 Ada R. Habershon, *The Study of Miracles* (Grand Rapids, MI: Kregal, 1957) 130.

Notice how Peter worded his statement. He did not say, "Wow, Jesus, look at You; I gotta try that." He asked Jesus to invite him onto the water. Peter had no intention of strolling on the lake minus the Master's beckon.

How does it fit here? It is a willingness to take chances, but only as directed and protected by God. Peter asked for an invitation. Jesus said, "Come." The word appeared so matter-of-factly, it seems Matthew reported a common event. Peter left the boat. Peter walked on the water to Jesus. He dared to leave the safety of the boat and walked toward His mentor.

> Peter, the experienced fisherman, who knew that the freshwater lake lacked even the partial buoyancy of the Dead Sea, left the boat. Amazed, the other disciples saw Peter walk toward Jesus. Then suddenly, Peter lost his nerve. He began to sink, and they heard a despairing cry, "Lord, save me!"[54]

If Peter's desire to walk on water stemmed from a hope of self-exaltation, scenes suddenly shifted that goal. Eyeing the waves and losing sight of Jesus, Peter sank. He cried for help in front of everyone. No time for precious words or formal prayers. He screamed, "Help!" Afraid and humbled, he expected that help. Peter rapidly fidgeted, facing this fact: without Christ he could do nothing.

---

54 John Pollock, *The Master* (Wheaton, IL: Victor Books, 1985) 97.

The Walk

Have you experienced that awareness? I have. Times when my weakness is obvious. Times when I have no ability on my own to solve a problem. Times when I struggle to say no to what I should say no to and say yes to what I should say yes to.

There are times—many times—when without Jesus I can do nothing.

I commended Peter for his willingness to take a risk. I applauded him for waiting for Christ's nod to come. Now, we might as well praise Peter's action again. As he began to sink, he certainly missed the security of the boat he departed. What did he do? He cried out to Jesus. Good move.

Why do I want to brag on that wet, afraid man? Maybe we could just say he had no other choice. Sorry to correct that view. But I know me too well. I know too many too well.

I've learned much through pastoring and counseling people who face difficult entanglements. They know Jesus. They know doctrine. Still, many stare at the waves. Many stubbornly refuse to call out to Jesus. Many refuse to do what they know to do, what they have taught others to do. They keep eyes on the water and battle with their own strength. They drown in disgusting independence.

I realize many difficulties are very deep, many storms are very harsh. A casual "keep your eyes on Jesus" won't correct serious psychological dysfunctions. On the other hand, we must not allow ourselves to delete Jesus from our therapy. The disciplines that focus our eyes on Jesus and solidify our dependency on

Him are not outdated. Prayer, Bible study, worship, service, and accountability cultivate our capacity to see Christ and depend on Him.

Peter didn't analyze the temperature of the water, the height of the waves or their distance from dry land. He was about to drown. So he cried for rescue.

Do we admit when we are sinking?

Jesus wants to rescue. He can offer help when we admit we need it.

Jesus did not delay. He reached and caught Peter. They climbed to the boat. When they were on board, the wind stopped. Jesus returned Peter to the safety of the boat and dealt with the original problem: the storm.

Notice the disciples' response. They worshipped Jesus. Their worship consisted of a confession: "Truly you are the Son of God." After the feast for five thousand, the people were satisfied. The disciples picked up the crumbs. Here, after a night of strife, they worshipped Jesus, recognizing His deity.

We love sunny days of miracles. We despise stormy nights of missing the boat. Can we, though, argue with the results? A long night ended in adoration for the Son of God.

Jesus started the evening by getting the disciples away from the crowd. Some lessons must be learned in darkness, away from noise—even religious noise. In silence Jesus reveals Himself to us in ways otherwise impossible. I usually forget that. Most of us long to mingle with multitudes, but Jesus habitually exited crowds to commune with His Father. Shouting and singing and sermonizing need to merge with silence.

That is the walk we can take, the walk Jesus invites us to take. On water. On shore. Wherever. Whenever. With Jesus, a walk in the sun or a walk through the storm.

When we enter the walk of silence we can move clearly. When we go boating at night in storming seas we can know we are not alone. When life is progressing with relative ease we will refuse the haughty lie that we are somehow capable apart from the Savior. When life slaps us hard we will refuse to tenaciously attempt to fight with our own strength. We will learn to cry "Help!" When drowning. And when sailing smoothly.

READ:

> Immediately Jesus made the disciples get into the boat and go on ahead of him to the other side, while he dismissed the crowd. After he had dismissed them, he went up on a mountainside by himself to pray. Later that night, he was there alone, and the boat was already a considerable distance from land, buffeted by the waves because the wind was against it.
>
> Shortly before dawn Jesus went out to them, walking on the lake. When the disciples saw him walking on the lake, they were terrified. "It's a ghost," they said, and cried out in fear.

But Jesus immediately said to them: "Take courage! It is I. Don't be afraid."

"Lord, if it's you," Peter replied, "tell me to come to you on the water."

"Come," he said.

Then Peter got down out of the boat, walked on the water and came toward Jesus. But when he saw the wind, he was afraid and, beginning to sink, cried out, "Lord, save me!"

Immediately Jesus reached out his hand and caught him. "You of little faith," he said, "why did you doubt?"

And when they climbed into the boat, the wind died down. Then those who were in the boat worshiped him, saying, "Truly you are the Son of God."

When they had crossed over, they landed at Gennesaret. And when the men of that place recognized Jesus, they sent word to all the surrounding country. People brought all their sick to him and begged him to let the sick just touch the edge of his cloak, and all who touched him were healed. (Matthew 14:22–36)

REFLECT:

1. In what way is Jesus saying to you: "Take courage. It is I?"

2. In what way is Jesus saying to you: "Do not be afraid?"

3. What is He asking you to walk through as He says, "Come?"

4. What are you asking Him to save you from as you ask Him to come?

RECEIVE:

What is it like when you stop, sit down, take a deep breath and look around you? What do you see, smell, feel, hear, taste? Does the culture's anesthesia wear off? —Susan S. Phillips[55]

55 Susan S. Phillips, *The Cultivated Life: From Ceaseless Striving to Receiving Joy* (Downers Grove, IL: InterVarsity Press, 2015) 79.

RESPOND:

- Think of ways your own walk with Jesus fits this story.
- Write about your fears, your doubts, and your dreams.
- Include Jesus in the story.
- What is He saying to you today?
- List ways He wants to guide your walk.

20

The Question

Matthew 20:26–28

> Sadly, our Christian worship services are of no help here. Today, for the most part, they have become one huge production in distraction.
> —Richard J. Foster[56]

"You didn't sound like your brain's all that damaged. You seemed fine to me."

After the lady said that to me, she began apologizing. She didn't think she stated her comment correctly. She talked more, making things worse as she tried to make it all better. "What I mean is, when I listened to you speak I had trouble believing you are so messed up."

---

56 Richard J. Foster, *Sanctuary of the Soul: Journey Into Meditative Prayer* (Downers Grove, IL: InterVarsity Press, 2011) 104–105.

After the "messed up" comment, her eyes opened wide and her skin turned red. She knew she was having trouble saying what she wanted to say.

But I laughed.

That's the best way to respond.

She laughed with me. I assured her that laughter helped. I wasn't offended at all by her effort to say, "You seem to be healthier than you really are." I actually like her version better that the sentence I just typed. And better than the medical report I still keep on file.

We were both attending a conference. The lady had heard me speak as I told the story of my own storm. The audience stared at images of my damaged brain on the screen—those who knew what they were seeing felt surprised that such victim could be the one talking. Externally, in my well-planned talk, on a podium as my place of comfort, within my own platform, maybe I seemed fine to her and others. But those who know me know I'm not always fine.

So, I just tell my story. About how my life changed and about how my life paused and about how Jesus was really there all the time even when the only evidence to prove it was faith— faith which didn't always bring feelings or good news or miracles along with it during our storm.

I didn't have a cool story to tell, like Peter. He could talk about walking on water and leave out the part about panicking.

The Question

He could tell about all the miracles he saw, being there in person to hear all the parables Jesus told, and knowing from experience the stories I'm reading and writing about.

Me? I haven't walked on water. I haven't seen a storm calm. I haven't stared at more bread and fish coming for the hungry crowd when we were sure we'd run out. I haven't seen the dead come back to life.

But I have stayed alive when I wasn't expected to live.

And that's the story I tell.

I tell a story about the swelling of my brain caused by encephalitis in March 1996. I tell a story of always-healthy-Chris getting sick, of being in the ER and almost dying, of spending days in the hospital, of not remembering the names of our three sons, of a nurse coming to our house three times a day after I was finally released, of being a man who communicated for a living then needing months of speech therapy. I tell a story about resulting brain damage, severe scar tissue throughout that damaged brain especially in my left temporal lobe, change in personality, radical mood swings, and now living with long term effects like epilepsy and short term memory issues and the need to nap. I tell a story about me, the fit husband and dad and pastor and coach, becoming the very sick me who tried very hard to be the former me but couldn't do most of what he'd done before. I tell of forgetting names, forgetting events, forgetting how to spell, and forgetting something else but I can't remember what. I tell of making things worse as I tried to make myself better.

That's the story I tell. That's the storm where the wind seems to still blow at times, the waves don't seem to ever fully calm at times, and the shore feels far, far away at times.

That's the story I tell—having trouble saying what I want to say. That's the story I live—as I reach for my meds, as I hold tightly to modern electronic devices that work to help my brain do her job a little better, as I stare while seeking a noun in my brain. That's the storm I feel around me, within me, surrounding me—when my story isn't sounding so fine to me.

How do I pause with Jesus holding tightly to that packed luggage? By actually realizing the phrase, "I can't do anything without Jesus," isn't a sermon title or a religious motto. It's a reality. It's my reality. I work hard to force this damaged brain to work. I follow the rules I've been given. I ask for help from others. But I can't do anything without Jesus.

Sorry if that phrase sounds childish to you. It is just the truth. I feel like a little kid in a not-so-young-man's body.

And that's another reason a story about how Jesus viewed children helps me feel a little better about everything. Even my damaged brain. Even my life with epilepsy. Even those things about me that I and others wish would not be as they are. This story lets me pause, crawl toward the smiling face of Jesus as I hear Him laugh, and let His muscular arms grab my weak self and cradle me to Himself.

There's a story of Jesus calling a child to the stage in response to His followers asking who would be the greatest in heaven.

This narrative isn't an isolated occurrence. Jesus addressed the pursuit of power several times. Once, the mother of James and John lobbied for her sons to hold high positions.[57] While it is motherly and innocent to want the best for a child, the lust for power can creep in. It did for her. When our responses to our children reflect more of how their behavior affects us than them, the serpent is slithering in the grass nearby.

Similar to that mom's request, this chapter's story begins with the disciples verbally sparring about rank in the Kingdom of Heaven. Competition. Promotion. Debate. Dispute. Such concerns, more familiar than I care to admit, reveal the hunger pains of humans craving for power.

Peter, James, and John had recently witnessed Jesus transfigured, speaking to Moses and Elijah. Not a normal day's work in my life. Then, Jesus drove an evil spirit from a boy and restored his health—a feat the disciples attempted but failed.

Jesus sent Peter to the lake to find money for taxes in the mouth of a fish. Talk about fodder for conversation.

They could have spoken of the greatest acts ever performed on earth, but they searched for a flow chart. No wonder James later wrote how church fights come from selfish ambitions.[58]

Jesus used their inquiry as a springboard for discourse, and invited a child to join them. With His live illustration at the center, Jesus told His circle of friends that they needed to

---

57 Matthew 20:20–21
58 James 4:1–3

change, to be "converted," to become like little children. If not, their dreams of entering the "kingdom" would never be realized. While they worried about the conditions they would find upon an arrival in Kingdom Land, Jesus spoke to them about requirements for entering.

We've probably heard about "becoming like a child." In the context of the story, Jesus made one point. We don't need to add more meanings; Christ's lesson is challenging enough: "Whoever humbles himself like this child is the greatest in the Kingdom of Heaven." The issue? Humility.

Maybe as nobodies, God can actually do through us what He longs to do. The New Testament analogy of the Body of Christ beautifully emphasizes how operational the church can be when made up of parts working together for the good of the whole. If we could grasp the awesome truth of our significance to Christ, we would be less likely to attempt proving our worth by becoming "somebodies" in the eyes of others.

The invitation from Christ is to be like the child.

I guess that's why I like this story so much. I am a man in need.

With my damaged brain and my driven self and my questions and my doubts and my love of Jesus, that's where I live. Like a kid walking His way, reaching for His hands, and hoping He will hold me again. Right now.

READ:

> At that time the disciples came to Jesus and asked,
> "Who is the greatest in the kingdom of heaven?"
>
> He called a little child, and placed the child among
> them. And he said: "I tell you the truth, unless you
> change and become like little children, you will never
> enter the kingdom of heaven. Therefore, whoever takes
> the lowly position of this child is the greatest in the
> kingdom of heaven" (Matthew 18:1–4).

REFLECT:

1. What personal weakness is part of your story?

2. What are some ways that a weakness could help you
   chase Christ like children pursing their greatest desires?

3. How would you answer the question, "Who is greatest
   in the Kingdom of Heaven?"

4. What are other practical ways of applying humility by
   choice in your life?

RECEIVE:

Our culture's preferred mode is anything but still. Constant work generates the impression of control and efficiency, holding at bay the mysterious while suppressing awareness of our own uncomfortable finitude. How much defensiveness against discomfort underlines both the neglect of sabbath keeping *and* the strict sabbath keeping that dodges relationship by focusing on rules and prohibitions? —Susan S. Phillips[59]

RESPOND:

- Think about your weakness.

- Place it in your list of objects that have the potential to help you run to Christ.

- Put together a plan to be sure you respond to your struggles by running to Christ like a child.

---

59 Susan S. Phillips, *The Cultivated Life: From Ceaseless Striving to Receiving Joy* (Downers Grove, IL: InterVarsity Press, 2015) 94.

21

The Choices

Luke 15:3–7

> It was a mixed crowd. It included Pharisees,
> social outcasts looking for friendship, sick folk
> hoping for healing, crowd chasers following
> the latest fad, and true disciples.
> —Leith Anderson[60]

I'm not the only one with a weakness. We all have some issues, don't we?

What are yours?

As we continue our experience of *Pause with Jesus,* we hope to not live in denial of our own stories. We seek to invite Jesus into our stories, or to realize He's invited Himself, and to respond to His guidance in our stories.

---

60 Leith Anderson, *Jesus: An Intimate Portrait of The Man, His Land, and His People* (Minneapolis, MN: Bethany House, 2005) 218.

But how does it really work? How can we take each of these chapters and fit them into our own expedition of grace, of redemption, of healing, of life with Christ?

For me, it helps to enter the stories. I believe in a loving God who welcomes me home—for dinner, for laughter, for an experience, for a conversation, for correction, for a nap. In these narratives written in an interesting mixture of styles from Matthew, Mark, Luke, and John, we find stories to learn. We read drama to keep. We read various moods and plots, all moving us toward time with Jesus.

And that's what these pages hope to do. Peek back. Gaze at ancient stories. Enter the creative nonfiction. Stay there. Learn there.

See how the lessons apply in the present. Grapple what the meaning in its original context is saying to us in our drive down the road in the rain, in our hustle to the grocery store one more time, in our wide awake late at night world of questions, in our staring at the news stories we wish weren't being told, in our desire to do the exact opposite of what we know we should do, in our moments when emotions aren't very pleasant toward another person, in our craving for one more bite of that unhealthy food.

Welcome the stories there. In those moments.

Not pushing them out of context—welcoming the context and inviting the large lesson to teach us. Inviting the larger lessons to take us to Jesus.

Not just stories about Him.

Experiences with Him.

Those encounters expose our weaknesses and reveal our battle with choices.

Through comments sent by friends when I asked about both their favorite stories of Jesus and their questions, I learned many of us have much in common. We ask similar questions. We battle similar wars. We carry similar wounds. We select similar favorites in the collection of Jesus stories. And we find similar stories hard to grasp.

In our mobile device/social media world, interesting remarks came my way.

But over and over, people confessed their love for the Prodigal Son. Maybe we should call the story the Lost Son since it is part of three-stories-to-make-a-point. Jesus was accused of spending time with "those people," and He didn't argue back. I can only imagine the expression on His face, but we can read all three of His stories.

If a sheep is lost what do you do? Find it. Get up, leave what is still there, and go find it.

If a coin is lost what do you do? Find it. Turn on the lights, move the furniture around, and go find it.

After those brief parables to make His point, Jesus told a story about a father and his two sons. The baby boy was ready to leave the family and live his own way. He asked his dad for inheritance and the father gave it all. The son left.

Jesus goes into detail here—not about time or distance, not including many of the things I wish He'd included, not letting the dad ask a few questions I think any father would ask—about the decision being a bad one.

The son received and left. The son lost it all and had very little choice for survival. So, he fought through his inner war and decided to give going home a try.

The dad wasn't waiting with a list of consequences.

The dad was waiting with a smile.

The dad didn't stay back seeking to make his son's return as difficult as possible.

The dad ran toward the son to meet him on the way. The dad called a party. The dad also had to help the oldest son realize staying home didn't give him any right to judge or hate or complain or fuss. It was time for everyone to party.

Notice the father's final words to the oldest son. Perfect lines to end the parable being heard by many older brothers and read by many judgmental, religious guys like me:

> "But we had to celebrate and be glad, because this brother of yours was dead and is alive again; he was lost and is found" (Luke 15:32).

Pause and consider the story. Do you feel like the lost son? Do you feel like the stay-at-home son? Do you feel like the dad? Do you feel like the tax collectors and sinners glad Jesus wants to spend time with you? Do you feel like the Pharisees and teachers of the law who muttered their complaints?

The Choices

It seems like each character in that drama needs to respond the same way. The lost son realized where he was, faced where he longed to be, and decided to go there.

Shouldn't each actor do that? A father, an older son, a younger son? A sinner, a teacher, a rule maker.

Me.

You.

Now.

Desires to leave. A need to stay home.

Desperation after leaving. A need to go back home.

A place of acceptance. A face of grace. A party to welcome your return.

Think about the story this way. Know where you are. Know where you long to be. Go there.

And let that place be home.

READ:

> Jesus continued: "There was a man who had two sons. The younger one said to his father, 'Father, give me my share of the estate.' So he divided his property between them.
>
> "Not long after that, the younger son got together all he had, set off for a distant country and there squandered his wealth in wild living. After he had spent everything,

there was a severe famine in that whole country, and he began to be in need. So he went and hired himself out to a citizen of that country, who sent him to his fields to feed pigs. He longed to fill his stomach with the pods that the pigs were eating, but no one gave him anything.

"When he came to his senses, he said, 'How many of my father's hired servants have food to spare, and here I am starving to death! I will set out and go back to my father and say to him: Father, I have sinned against heaven and against you. I am no longer worthy to be called your son; make me like one of your hired servants.' So he got up and went to his father.

"But while he was still a long way off, his father saw him and was filled with compassion for him; he ran to his son, threw his arms around him and kissed him.

"The son said to him, 'Father, I have sinned against heaven and against you. I am no longer worthy to be called your son.'

"But the father said to his servants, 'Quick! Bring the best robe and put it on him. Put a ring on his finger and sandals on his feet. Bring the fattened calf and kill it. Let's have a feast and celebrate. For this son of mine was dead and is alive again; he was lost and is found.' So they began to celebrate.

"Meanwhile, the older son was in the field. When he came near the house, he heard music and dancing. So he called one of the servants and asked him what was going on. 'Your brother has come,' he replied, 'and your father has killed the fattened calf because he has him back safe and sound.'

"The older brother became angry and refused to go in. So his father went out and pleaded with him. But he answered his father, 'Look! All these years I've been slaving for you and never disobeyed your orders. Yet you never gave me even a young goat so I could celebrate with my friends. But when this son of yours who has squandered your property with prostitutes comes home, you kill the fattened calf for him!'

"'My son,' the father said, 'you are always with me, and everything I have is yours. But we had to celebrate and be glad, because this brother of yours was dead and is alive again; he was lost and is found.'" (Luke 15:11–32)

REFLECT:

1. What are your two favorite stories about Jesus?

2. How do you feel about the story often called the Prodigal Son?

3. What part do you see yourself playing in that drama?

4. What choices should you make to return home?

5. How can you help others feel welcome as they return home?

RECEIVE:

The parable of the prodigal son, especially, tears down my neat categories that separate responsible from irresponsible, obedient from rebellious, moral from immoral. Such is grace. —Philip Yancey[61]

RESPOND:

- Slowly read the story of the Lost Son.
- Imagine each part of the parable, and evaluate your own role in the story.

---

61 Philip Yancey, *Vanishing Grace: Whatever Happened to the Good News?* (Grand Rapids, MI: Zondervan, 2014) 52.

The Choices

- Read the parable of the lost sheep and the parable of the lost coin Jesus told in that setting (Luke 15).

- Understand the context of Jesus being accused of welcoming sinners and eating with them.

- Pray as you contemplate the stories.

22

The Worry

Luke 15:8–10

Do you feel a need for affirmation? Does your self-esteem need attention? You don't need to drop names and show off. You need only pause at the base of the cross and be reminded of this: The maker of the stars would rather die for you than live without you. And that is a fact. So if you need to brag, brag about that.
—Max Lucado[62]

we are moving forward through the ancient roads and homes,

through the historical events and conflict,

through the miracles and division,

we are moving.

---

62 Max Lucado, *Traveling Light: Releasing the Burdens You Were Never Intended to Bear* (Nashville, TN: W Publishing Group, 2001) 77.

and that, yes, is the goal.

to move. to no longer remain just as we are.

to move;

not to impress or earn love,

but in response to love received

that could never be earned.

moved by such love,

that is unconditional, and more than real.

we are still and going, sure and afraid,

not knowing about these moves.

to move,

not as a means of escaping moments of displeasure

but rather

to realize deeper value, hidden treasure, noisy silence, busy stillness

amid the rapid rituals of hurry and competition and lies and wounds.

to move,

toward rather than away,

with rather than without,

near rather than from a distance.

but, even in this,

The Worry

all of this,

all of this good news

of hope and forgiveness and compassion,

worry visits us.

doesn't she visit you?

i know i

am told not to worry,

that all will be fine,

that we win in the end.

my voice states such phrases

and my hands type similar sentences

and my deep heart believes their truth

while my thoughts and feelings seem to be held by

a little or

much worry

too often.

so, in the middle of that tension

i have a choice.

will i think about Jesus and sing about Jesus and write about
Jesus

or will i

invite Jesus into my worry?

it helps me to visit His story

and His many stories

as i invite Him to my story

and my many stories.

my stories of worry—

in all her shapes and colors; with all her masks and covers—

are real stories of my own inner self

and real stories of you and them, of here and there

as we seem to put forth so much effort and muscle

to prove our false selves to be real

amid the debates and hates of talks and rules

about us against someone somewhere else.

i worry as a reality of us.

but also

i listen, at least i try to listen,

and learn, at least i hope to learn,

as i

read words

from that voice so real, so good, so true.

He said to them and He says to me

The Worry

words and sentences and stories of peace,
of rest, of trust, of hope.
He instructs me to investigate my worry.
am i seeking to accomplish something
in a personal desire for applause?
am i dwelling on a few sentences, a few phrases
which appear doable and attainable and reachable,
which seem to carry value and bring applause
while i'm actually missing the big story,
the larger story,
the true story,
of what i say i really believe anyway?
before we go forward
any farther with Christ,
any farther with ourselves,
any farther with our dreams,
we are to travel backward
again to
hear Christ's sermon
again to
see Christ's words

again to

allow time for our story to be edited

and redirected toward healing.

worry often holds us too tightly.

to defeat her hold

we must notice her hold

while also noticing greater stories we've been told,

greater stories we're becoming

while moving from stories of past

deception and defeat and poor decisions

toward a new moving of motion

in a story

which ends so

well.

READ:

> "Therefore I tell you, do not worry about your life, what you will eat or drink; or about your body, what you will wear. Is not life more than food, and the body more than clothes? Look at the birds of the air; they do not sow or reap or store away in barns, and yet your

heavenly Father feeds them. Are you not much more valuable than they? Can any one of you by worrying add a single hour to your life?

"And why do you worry about clothes? See how the flowers of the field grow. They do not labor or spin. Yet I tell you that not even Solomon in all his splendor was dressed like one of these. If that is how God clothes the grass of the field, which is here today and tomorrow is thrown into the fire, will he not much more clothe you—you of little faith? So do not worry, saying, 'What shall we eat?' or 'What shall we drink?' or 'What shall we wear?' For the pagans run after all these things, and your heavenly Father knows that you need them. But seek first his kingdom and his righteousness, and all these things will be given to you as well. Therefore do not worry about tomorrow, for tomorrow will worry about itself. Each day has enough trouble of its own" (Matthew 6:25–34).

REFLECT:

1. What do you worry about most often?

2. What is Christ saying to you as He gently invites you away from worry?

3. What practical steps can you take to obey Him?

4. Who do you have who can help you?

RECEIVE:

> For people, like so many Samaritans then and so many Americans now, who don't even know there is a story, Jesus, patiently and without raising his voice, tells story after story after story. Stories that get us into The Story.
> —Eugene H. Peterson[63]

RESPOND:

- Write a poem about your worry.
- Realize the larger story of your life and refuse to let portions of the story control you.
- Spend time with a dear friend.
- Pray together and ask Jesus to help you say goodbye to unnecessary worry.

---

63 Eugene H. Peterson, *Tell It Slant: A Conversation on the Language of Jesus in His Stories and Prayers* (Grand Rapids, MI: Wm. B. Eerdmans Publishing Co, 2008) 121.

23

The Cry

Luke 18:1–8

> It is quite natural in prayer to ask wrongly or
> not at all. We must learn to ask, and to ask
> rightly. —Timothy Keller[64]

Jesus had just finished lecturing the disciples about the dangers of pride. Then He walked into a crowd. People pushed for a chance to see that Man whose reputation preceded Him. They glanced, stared, listened, and walked in His direction. Suddenly a cry could be heard above the clamor.

The voice? A beggar.

The purpose? He hoped that popular leader would hear him.

His plea? A shout for mercy.

Pride didn't cloak his insecurities. Bartimaeus, the blind beggar, had no one to impress. Pleading in desperation, he cried

---

64 Timothy Keller, *Prayer*, 223.

for a cure. He refused to clothe his nervousness with courtesy. Maybe he told himself his day had come. Maybe that would be his final chance to find change.

How often do our hurting hearts incorrectly assume that, since God knows everything anyway, time shouldn't be wasted by praying and pleading? Sincerely not wishing to order God—as some seem to enjoy attempts of—the reluctance goes the opposite way.

Refusing to treat Almighty God as a cosmic bellhop is a good thing. But failing to pray doesn't fit my reading of these stories. It distances the needy from His hands. In these narratives I hear an invitation, a welcome, a summons. I hear Christ saying, "Come to me. Ask me."

Like Bartimaeus, we do not fully see. We lack much. We are beggars. Unlike Bartimaeus, we refuse to cry frantically for God to rescue us.

Prayer permits us to admit our helplessness. It allows us to participate in the movement of God. Allowed to join God in seeing His work accomplished? Yes, I confess, the plot doesn't seem to all fit together when we take the risky belief that an omnipotent (all-powerful) and omniscient (all-knowing) Creator often waits for our cry before taking action.

Crowds of beggars walked past Jesus. Many chose to remain where they were, as they were, refusing to howl for help. Bartimaeus cried until Jesus could hear him.

The Cry

Where are we in that drama? Have we found our little spot—hurrying through life while carrying our hurt with us as we go? Or will we cry for a rescue, for a release, for a relationship with the True Lover?

Bartimaeus lacked courtesy. Jesus, busy and in constant demand, stood in the middle of a large audience. He needed to leave that city and be about His Father's business. An interruption by a neighborhood street bum's screams fell under the heading of unnecessary demands on the already overworked Messiah. His friends, family, the denominational committee and the neighborhood watch commission voted to veto his screams. Their schemes would not allow such a distraction.

What should happen next? What should happen when crowds disapprove of what our souls crave? The Bartimaeus in us should keep believing. When told to silence our effort to have a little faith, the Bartimaeus in us must shout even more—whatever our effort of shouting might be.

The more acute the condition, the less the crying one cares what others think. Bartimaeus continued crying out. His vision overlooked the critics. His hopes rested in Christ alone.

Frederick Buechner applauds such tenacity:

> According to Jesus, by far the most important thing about praying is to keep at it. The images he uses to explain this are all rather comic, as though he thought it was rather comic to have to explain it at all. He says God is like a friend you go to borrow bread from at midnight.

The friend tells you in effect to drop dead, but you go on knocking anyway until finally he gives you what you want so he can go back to bed again (Luke 11:5–8). Or God is like a crooked judge who refuses to hear the case of a certain poor widow, presumably because he knows there's nothing much in it for him. But she keeps on hounding him until finally he hears her case just to get her out of his hair (Luke 18:1–8). Even a stinker, Jesus says, won't give his own son a black eye when he asks for peanut butter and jelly, so how all the more will God when his children (Matthew 7:9–11). Be importunate, Jesus says—not one assumes because you have to beat a path to God's door before he'll open it, but because until you beat the path maybe there's no way of getting to your door.[65]

Jesus paused. He turned toward those keeping a block between the shouter and the Listener, and said, "Call him."

Though Christ planned to journey to Jerusalem for the Passover, He took time for a beggar. He refused to pass him over.

Those who told Bartimaeus to hush, hurried to shift their views. "Cheer up! On your feet! He's calling you," they declared.

---

65 Frederick Buechner, *Wishful Thinking* (San Francisco: Harper & Row, 1973) 70–71.

The Cry

Bartimaeus heard their words, left cool composure behind, darted to his feet, tossed off his outer garment, and raced to Jesus.

I think of one word here: desperation!

I think that is a word and a reality we prefer to ignore, to deny, to misinterpret. We feel desperate but tend to respond incorrectly. We prefer to hide it under the stack of our efforts and labor and goals and agenda.

I pray I become more like Bartimaeus. Instead of running away, I pray I run toward. Instead of a casual stroll, sometimes I might just need my pause to be a race toward Jesus. Through the crowds of my own doubts, past the distractions of my self-talk, beyond obstruction from poor decisions I've made, I need to run toward Jesus.

Not to escape. To enter.

Not to seek a momentary high. To pursue healing.

With anticipation, Bartimaeus scurried to the side of the Savior with expectant faith.

When Bartimaeus arrived, Jesus asked, "What do you want me to do?"

Bartimaeus did not want sympathy. He did not crave attention. He did not seek pity that would provide a framework for owning a distinct identity. Bartimaeus wanted one thing. To be healed. He said, "Rabbi, I want to see." Short. Direct. To the point. That is a way to pray.

Long litanies overflowing with elegant words? Not required. An honest, desperate cry for a specific need.

Maybe today's prayer requests should be just that.

Each book in the *pause* series emphasizes prayer. Sometimes those prayers are just getting to the point. Other times, when we have no specific words to voice, lingering in God's presence and enjoying Him is fine. Letting Him speak to us is good. Listening and learning through various spiritual methods of communicating with Jesus are all good.

But sometimes we should just ask to see.

With reverence but without hesitation. With desperation but without elaboration.

Jesus asked. Bartimaeus answered by asking to see.

Jesus then told the beggar to go. He did not give specific direction, saying, "Be on your way." Christ's command included a benefit, "Your faith has healed you."

What had happened? "Immediately he received his sight and followed Jesus down the road."

What if Bartimaeus had remained in the rut of his begging, never venturing out in faith? What if the crowd's objections had deterred him from pursuing Jesus with tenacity? What if he had stopped at any point along the way?

Are we afraid to cry out? Is it hard to admit utter helplessness? What obstacles deter our pursuit? Do memories of unanswered prayers in the past paralyze dreams in the present?

Pray. Call out to God in desperation.

Beg and plead. Intercede. Those cries are fine.

The Listening Doctor can choose to bless beggars like us on days like today.

READ:

> Then they came to Jericho. As Jesus and his disciples, together with a large crowd, were leaving the city, a blind man, Bartimaeus (which means "Son of Timaeus"), was sitting by the roadside begging. When he heard that it was Jesus of Nazareth, he began to shout, "Jesus, Son of David, have mercy on me!"
>
> Many rebuked him and told him to be quiet, but he shouted all the more, "Son of David, have mercy on me!"
>
> Jesus stopped and said, "Call him."
>
> So they called to the blind man, "Cheer up! On your feet! He's calling you." Throwing his cloak aside, he jumped to his feet and came to Jesus.
>
> "What do you want me to do for you?" Jesus asked him.
>
> The blind man said, "Rabbi, I want to see."
>
> "Go," said Jesus, "your faith has healed you." Immediately he received his sight and followed Jesus along the road. (Mark 10:46–52)

REFLECT:

1. How can you cry to Christ for a specific need?

2. What or who seems to be standing in the way?

3. Are you willing to walk through that hindrance?

4. What cloak should you throw aside to move forward with your healing?

RECEIVE:

What about the boy who is not healed? When, listened to or not listened to, the prayer goes unanswered? Who knows? Just keep praying, Jesus says. Remember the sleepy friend, the crooked judge. Even if the boy dies, keep on beating the path to God's door, because the one thing you can be sure of is that down the path you beat even with your most half-cocked and halting prayer the God you call upon will finally come, and even if he does not bring you the answer you want, he

will bring you himself. And maybe at the secret heart of all our prayers that is what we are really praying for.
—Frederick Buechner[66]

RESPOND:

- Realize your present need.
- Pursue Christ and His healing.
- Refuse to be stopped in your journey.
- Pray specifically.

---

66 Frederick Buechner, *Wishful Thinking*, 70–71.

24

The Climb

Luke 19:10

> Success sabotages the memories of the successful. Kings of the mountain forget who carried them up the trail. —Max Lucado[67]

For Zacchaeus, life as usual consisted of a nice income linked to a terrible social life. As the chief tax collector, people enjoyed seeing him show up about as much as a famine. He could pay his bills and have money left over. He headed the district collection of taxes for the Romans with a job that kept food on his table and friends at a distance. Crookedness was as much a part of the vocation as the needed knowledge of accounting.

When that "sawed off little social disaster"[68] heard Jesus was going to be traveling in his direction, he reacted with zeal. He did not have friends or a good reputation, but he knew one thing.

---

67 Max Lucado, *It's Not About Me: Rescue from the Life We Thought Would Make Us Happy* (Brentwood, TV: Integrity Publishing, 2004) 134.
68 Frederick Buechner, *Peculiar Treasures,* 180.

Zacchaeus wanted to see the Man he regularly heard about. He wanted to see who Jesus was or what He was or what He could do for him.

Sometimes our pause with Jesus involves action. A step. A leap. A dive. A climb. A dinner together.

A mom informs a Son to bring in some wine. One lady reaches to barely touch a Healer. Another lady washes His feet with expensive oil. Peter had to venture out of a boat onto tumultuous water. Friends break a roof to drop down their friend so Christ can bring him healing. Bartimaeus had to cry loudly to be heard above the commotion.

Zacchaeus wanted to see Jesus. If he wanted it badly enough, he had to do something about it.

My pause and your pause today might include a climb we normally refuse to take.

We can hope of drawing near to Jesus, but the fulfillment of that hunger will lie dormant until we take action. Zacchaeus' desire to see Jesus began to move toward fulfillment when he took action.

A short guy climbing a tree to see over the heads of a crowd intrigues us. Discouragement over his stature and the size of a crowd could have derailed the pursuit of his dream. Zacchaeus did not let that stop him; his determination overruled his dilemma. He implemented his plan of seeing Jesus by climbing the now famous sycamore tree.

Jesus arrived and looked up to see what must have been a comical sight as Zacchaeus watched from his perch: a wealthy, friendless, short guy roosting in a tree, determined to see Jesus passing by. The watcher got more than he expected. Notice the words Christ spoke to him:

"Zacchaeus," Jesus chuckles, "What are you doing up there? Come down here and let's get lunch."

I could laugh if I didn't see so much of us in the drama.

Zacchaeus came down and took Jesus to his house. The short man's life changed.

The religious folks didn't care for Christ's new friend but Christ didn't care much for their opinions. The reason? Because Jesus cared for Zacchaeus. For one man. For one tiny man willing to climb a tree and take a glance at a Friend walking by.

I imagine the scene. I consider others who were gazing at Jesus, at Zacchaeus, at the facial expressions of others. I wonder what character I resemble the most.

Stories like this invite me back to the bigger story. They help me work through my own shortness and find a place to gain a better view. I don't want to stand, watch, reach conclusions, and do nothing.

I want Jesus to come over. What should I do? How can I climb better to place myself in His sight?

I need to pause this way sometimes: find the nearest tree and climb to the top. Maybe I climb by studying a commentary on a biblical text, by singing an ancient hymn I could hardly understand when hearing it as a young child, by meditating on a modern song that might seem a little too feel-good-for-some but actually could be just what I need for my climb, by refusing to rush the climb but slowly meditating on an creed agreed upon by many denominations, by praying for a miracle, by reading a creative book to expand my damaged brain that God still has plans for, by writing a poem, by staring at nature, by seeing a person beside me hoping to climb also and choosing to help them join me in seeing Jesus.

If we need to see Jesus better, let's do whatever we must to gain a glance. No inconvenience is too tall.

Does that frighten you?

A friend said to me, "I think Jesus says to us, 'How much of Me do you want? How close do you want to be?' It can be scary." Or as Donald Miller's book title reminds us: *Scary Close.*

I agree with my friend. But I am also too scared to not get close.

Let's be scared enough to not miss a moment with Jesus as He comes into our towns of thoughts and time and life and crisis and relationships and lies and lust and deception and politics and dreams and vision and wounds and scars and church and hope and disagreements and medication. Let's be scared enough to refuse to neglect an opportunity. Let's be scared enough with the right kind of fear—lured toward a love that doesn't match our own script but travels past it on the way to our hearts. Let's be scared enough to climb a tree, to bend a knee, to close our eyes, to open our ears, to sing a song, to forgive an enemy, to find a friend, to whisper a prayer.

Jesus is passing through town.

Invite Him over for lunch.

READ:

> Jesus entered Jericho and was passing through. A man was there by the name of Zacchaeus; he was a chief tax collector and was wealthy. He wanted to see who Jesus was, but because he was short man he could not see over the crowd. So he ran ahead and climbed a sycamore-fig tree to see him, since Jesus was coming that way.
>
> When Jesus reached the spot, he looked up and said to him, "Zacchaeus, come down immediately. I must stay at your house today." So he came down at once and welcomed him gladly.
>
> All the people saw this and began to mutter, "He has gone to be the guest of a sinner."
>
> But Zacchaeus stood up and said to the Lord, "Look, Lord! Here and now I give half of my possessions to the poor, and if I have cheated anybody out of anything, I will pay back four times the amount."
>
> Jesus said to him, "Today salvation has come to this house, because this man, too, is a son of Abraham. For the Son of Man came to seek and to save the lost" (Luke 19:1–10).

REFLECT:

1. What is your favorite part of the story about Zacchaeus? Why?

2. What are ways you can "climb a tree" to see Jesus better?

3. How would you feel if Jesus came to your house for dinner?

RECEIVE:

Of course, in our human condition we aren't always able to put our minds and hearts on the path of Christ. But we know that these ripples on the surface of our souls cannot become tidal waves when we descend into the inner sanctum of our graced selves and enter into the prayer of listening to our God, who reminds us, "Quiet your heart and be still. I am with you. Do not be afraid. I hold you in the palm of my hand. All is well." —Brennan Manning[69]

---

69 Brennan Manning, *The Importance of Being Foolish: How to Think Like Jesus* (San Francisco: HarperSanFransico, 2005) 95.

RESPOND:

- Take action—not to seek approval and applause from God and not to seek to impress Him.
- Take action to invest yourself in getting to know Him better.
- Make a list of ways you can "climb a tree."
- Write a story about Jesus coming over to your house for dinner.

25

The Honesty

Luke 20:19

Disciples of Jesus, beware of cute. Christians
are on high alert for cute. We love cuteness.
This is a cute-driven culture. It turns everything
it touches into glitz and attractiveness
and gets rid of anything that isn't "cute."
—Leonard Sweet and Frank Viola[70]

The story of Zacchaeus ends well. The drama and tension
tempt us to smile. We like the conflict and we take the side of
the winners.

But when we pause with Jesus, we need to snatch a thorny
truth. Not all these gospel stories are happy, happy, happy. I like
to see the smile of Jesus. To me, that is a face often missing in

---

70 Leonard Sweet and Frank Viola, *Jesus Manifesto: Restoring
the Supremacy and Sovereignty of Jesus Chris* (Nashville, TN:
Thomas Nelson, 2010) 75.

our culture, our churches, our minds, our souls, our stories. I must be honest, though, and admit this: not every story portrays Jesus smiling.

That shouldn't lure us back to hateful sermons where insecure preachers try to prove themselves as powerful by verbally and emotionally pushing and shoving until hell feels right below the pews—or, possibly near the pulpit. That shouldn't prompt us forward to a new generational attempt to overcompensate mediocrity by theologically and politically tempting and luring audiences toward incorrect extremes. But we should welcome the luring and prompting of Jesus to invite us to pause and hear Him—whether we like His words or not. Only then do we fully know Him. Only then do we truly pause and grow—maybe slowly, maybe slightly—into a better, deeper, more real relationship with our Mentor.

When we hang out with Jesus, we might notice His love for the very people who are against Him.

Not all the gospel narratives cause me to smile. The Passion Week—that journey from Palm Sunday through Good Friday to Resurrection Day—ends well but includes sadness, pain, questions, death. And many other stories before that week also bring tension just as we study them. Stories Jesus told. Responses from audiences.

Did Jesus really say that He came to bring a sword? Did He really say to let the dead bury the dead, to gouge out my eyes when they look at someone with lust, to sell everything I own, to eat His flesh and drink His blood? I have read each story often, trying to be sure they say only what I want them to mean. They don't always take my side. Books like *The Hard Sayings of Jesus* by F.F. Bruce and others help me understand His comments better. But they also leave me aware of this: Jesus cares too much to only say what we want to hear.

I pause to learn from Him, not just to nod. I pause to be changed, not just to be sure He didn't forget me.

I thought again about those stories as I sat at breakfast with my friend Greg Amos. Greg had recently been studying some of Christ's most tough-to-receive statements. He said,

> Imagine how challenging it must have been for the disciples to hear Jesus state that unless they eat His flesh and drink His blood they have no life in them.[71] Had He lost His mind? One could easily see how the concept of cannibalism would be forbidden. Or when sweet Jesus got upset that His Father's house had lost its God-given-purpose as a house of prayer and had, instead, become a den of thieves. Quite a contrast both of Jesus' violent response here versus other situations as well as His description of a den of thieves. Jesus had plenty of occasions to get upset, even violent, but chose not to. A den of thieves is the place where thieves or "sinners" go to hide out and feel safe from being convicted of their sin.

71 John 6:53

Greg was talking about the very stories I didn't want to include in this book. I'd rather pick the stories—and choose segments of the stories—I prefer. Pausing to hear Christ correct me, confront me, and compare me to goats doesn't inspire me to rest beside still waters. Those stories tend to be overused for incorrect reasons or left out all together.

But those stories are all parts of the story.

We must pause to hear Jesus—in all that He says. Not just crafting what we wish He had said or what we would prefer that He is saying now.

Love tells us the truth. For the right reasons and with pure motives, love does that. Just like Jesus did.

Greg explained the heart of Christ's love even in those stories:

> Once in preparing my heart for leading the congregation in Holy Communion, I sat on the front row reading my Bible. As many churches do, we had a communion table down front. When my eyes fell on the inscription, "This do in remembrance of me" leapt in my spirit. It was as if I could hear the Lord saying with intensity, "Remember Me!" The eating of His flesh and drinking of His blood, as we understand, shows His death and resurrection until He comes. He was giving us in those cannibalistic overtones an impressionable reminder of the act and meaning of Holy Communion. Us in Him and Him in us.

His cleansing of the temple was an expression of His disgust at how the people of God misrepresent God to the world. Jesus was getting ready to close out the season of His earthly ministry and, in my opinion, set a pattern. I believe He has begun to do the same before He closes out this season and returns. He will return for a glorious church. No spots, no wrinkles. A gorgeous bride whom He has made ready and has made herself ready. He comes by His Father's house individually and corporately to remind us where we too have allowed our lives and the church to misrepresent Him. The cleansing is not for destruction but rather for a purifying and setting in order for the wedding to come.

Love can be very honest, can't it?

Jesus can be very honest, can't He?

Today, maybe we are the temples He is cleansing. Let's welcome the purification.

READ:

You have heard that it was said, "Love your neighbor and hate your enemy." But I tell you, love your enemies and pray for those who persecute you, that you may be children of your Father in heaven. He causes his sun

to rise on the evil and the good, and sends rain on the righteous and the unrighteous. If you love those who love you, what reward will you get?
(Matthew 5:43–46a)

REFLECT:

1. What comments from Jesus are the most difficult for you to receive?

2. As you work to understand the true meaning of those words, how do they apply in your life?

3. What difficult words is He saying to you right now?

4. How should you respond?

RECEIVE:

I know my tendency is to rush over these familiar but difficult stories or the familiar sayings of Jesus. It is easy for me to read in such a way that I never really enter the story. I don't allow myself to be confronted. I don't hear the teaching of Jesus in a way that is fresh.

—George H. Guthrie[72]

RESPOND:

- Read the difficult stories of Christ.
- Study to understand their true meaning in the original context.
- Learn how that applies in your life.
- Receive the honesty from the One who loves you deeply.

---

72 George H. Guthrie, *Read the Bible for Life: Your Guide to Understanding & Living God's Word* (Nashville, TN: B & H Publishing Group, 2011) 178.

26

The Week

Luke 19:37–38

> In a time-honored act of welcome to royalty, the people lay their robes on the ground. This forms the carpet due a king. Overhead, the people wave branches they have just torn from trees. They are "preparing the way," demonstrating to this man that they receive him as their ruler. —Stephen Mansfield[73]

As we look at firm comments of Christ, we must keep them in the large context of His mission. They are parts of the story. Christ's story. Our stories.

This chapter highlights a week in His life that moved so many components of the story toward a revelation of that mission. This chapter reminds us to glance back in time as the

---

73 Stephen Mansfield, *Killing Jesus: The Unknown Conspiracy Behind the World's Most Famous Execution* (Brentwood, TN: Worthy Publishing, 2013) 54.

Strong One became weak, as the God-Man intentionally gives up His superman cape, as followers applaud then seek to crucify, as politics and religion are nothing new, as love really does lie bleeding.

Engage in the moments of this week. Place yourself in the scenes. Embrace the tension of history. Welcome that tension into your present story.

How? By letting a reading of Christ entering a city become more that historical Palm Sunday. Allow that past tradition to inspire true, genuine worship. Sing and celebrate, walk and run, stare and imagine, all while marveling in His presence. Invite His entrance into the town of your calendar, the cities of your relationships, the metropolis of your thoughts, the valley of your emotions.

Study into the history of that event—reading and research as time with Jesus.

Be still and meditate on the historical moment—silence and contemplation as time with Jesus.

Read the entire context of Jesus entering town—use a variety of translations and commentaries. Journal your own thoughts and feelings. Remember times of celebrating Christ. Think of times you should have but didn't.

Continue thinking about the week. Jesus taking His two-mile journey from Jerusalem to Bethany—what were His thoughts? Jesus as He fell asleep; Jesus as He woke in the morning—how do those memories make you feel? Jesus protesting in the temple, arguing with chief priests, announcing His death, debating with religious leaders—learn more about Him in each of those incidents.

Read the words Christ spoke. Read about the greatest commandment.

Take time to read of Judas signing a contract to betray Jesus. Stay a while in that scene.

And let the story guide you as you think and pray and study and learn. Let each segment of the drama remind you, confront you, hurt you, and heal you.

Hear Jesus calling religious leaders hypocrites and snakes.

Hear Jesus crying about Jerusalem's rejection.

Hear conversations with Christ and His followers at their Passover meal.

What if you had been in those scenes with them? What can you learn from them in your present chapter of life?

Visit the Garden of Gethsemane—listen to His prayer.

Visit the outward part of the Garden—observe His arrest.

What does that mean to us today, now? How should our lives be affected by that historical week? How can these weeks in our hurried world slow a bit and let us recall the face of Christ staring at His accusers, glancing at His denier, as He felt such deep pain from punishment He never deserved.

Listen to joyful songs about His entrance into a city.

Listen to painful songs about His death on a cross.

Shout and celebrate. Think of Jesus entering your own town. Select a song you would want to hear playing as He walked by. Visualize His facial expression as He made eye contact with you. Notice your city and weep for the wounded hearts. Receive Communion in silence. Apologize for denying Him. Stare at the crowds against Him.

And choose.

Choose this week to learn from that week.

Choose this week to live like Christ.

He saw more than religious eyes could see. He heard more than addicted ears could here.

He loved more than anyone has ever loved.

Can't we respond to His love?

> It is a love response to the ultimate love gift of God for us personally in Jesus. He lays down his life out of love so that we might live in love again. How can we not respond?[74]

Lays His life down?

For us?

Because of love?

For love?

---

74 John Michael Talbot, *The Jesus Prayer: A Cry for Mercy, A Path of Renewal* (Downers Grove, IL: InterVarsity Press, 2013) 112.

The Week

As I read this story I can think of ways I've been inspired by it. I can let that be all.

Or I can let now be the moment I enter that week with Jesus. My Sundays and Mondays and Tuesdays and Wednesdays and Thursdays can be more than days. They can be moments of spiritual formation. Instead of enduring the days, I can experience Christ in the days. Instead of rushing toward a weekend, I can notice a crowd and love a betrayer and eat with a few friends and cry in the dark.

Those can be moments with Jesus.

Not needing to dress a particular way or to feel stimulating emotions. Not needing to fully understand every detail before believing its reality. Not needing to fit with any tribe, no matter how deeply I long to. Not needing to have never failed to applaud His entrance or to meet Jesus for dinner, but realizing today is a new day and a new chance to see Him yourself.

Those can be moments with Jesus.

Real moments. New moments. Deep moments. Exciting moments. Calm moments. Joyful moments. Peaceful moments.

Books and movies reveal more about that week in the life of Jesus. So do our faces, our conversations, our attitudes. By visiting with Jesus every week we can "live in love again."

READ:

> When he came near the place where the road goes down the Mount of Olives, the whole crowd of disciples began joyfully to praise God in loud voices for all the miracles they had seen:
>
> "Blessed is the king who comes in the name of the Lord!"
>
> "Peace in heaven and glory in the highest!"
>
> Some of the Pharisees in the crowd said to Jesus, "Teacher, rebuke your disciples!"
>
> "I tell you," he replied, "if they keep quiet, the stones will cry out."
>
> As he approached Jerusalem and saw the city, he wept over it and said, "If you, even you, had only known on this day what would bring you peace—but now it is hidden from your eyes. The days will come upon you when your enemies will build an embankment against you and encircle you and hem you in on every side. They will dash you to the ground, you and the children within your walls. They will not leave one stone on another, because you did not recognize the time of God's coming to you." (Luke 19:39–44)

REFLECT:

1. How do you relate to celebrating Christ?

2. How do you feel about His weeping?

3. What are your thoughts about His conflict with the religious leaders?

4. What does this week's story say to you personally?

RECEIVE:

We do not become less needy, less dependent when we pray; we become more needy, more dependent—which is to say, more human. When we pray we dive ever more deeply into the very human condition from which sin alienates us and Christ saves us. —Eugene H. Peterson[75]

---

75 Eugene H. Peterson, *Tell It Slant: A Conversation on the Language of Jesus in His Stories and Prayers* (Grand Rapids, MI: Wm. B. Eerdmans Publishing Co, 2008) 55.

RESPOND:

- Travel slowly through each of the practices suggested through this chapter.

- Apply the disciplines as methods to pause with Jesus.

- Don't miss the opportunity to let the historical week become spiritually transformational in your life.

- Don't remain quiet and allow the stones to cry out.

27

The Night

Matthew 26:46

> Our regular participation in the Lord's Supper in the meantime is meant to make us hunger all the more as we wait for the meal that lies ahead, when God's personal presence, God's just reign and God's perfect peace will be realized in their fullness. —Barry D. Jones[76]

He walked on the water.

He took the hand of a dead girl and lifted her to life.

He fed thousands,

yet always made time for the few.

the people loved Him and hated Him. marching through life,

propelled by Love, filled with Truth, radiating Glory,

---

76 Barry D. Jones, *Dwell: Life with God for the World* (Downers Grove, IL: InterVarsity Press, 2014) 155.

Jesus edged ever closer to His death with each holy step.

by caring for sinners and confronting saints

He left detractors little option;

they could erase Him or exalt Him, they could give their lives to Him

or discover a way to take away His.

that night, the drama of His destiny began beating. loudly. closely.

hearing its relentless cadence, His inner world grew dark;

darker than the unusually dark world around Him on this night.

yes, He was God. yes, He was man. He knew

of the purpose, of the plan. yet, He felt.

He felt deeply.

maybe to help relieve His pain,

maybe to help them learn to feel true pain, He invited His disciples.

so many invitations,

but this one was unique. He called them,

these He had experienced life with for three adventurous years,

He called them to the garden.

deeper into darkness. deeper into His pain.

deep in prayer with His Father.

then, He called three to go all the way with Him:

peter. james. john.

He invited them to agony. not joy.

not to gratification and gain. to emptiness, to loneliness.

troubled, full of sorrow, He walked. this God-Man looked, sounded, much more man,

much less God.

voicing His pain in candid words,

His honesty kicked all pretensions aside, admitting sorrow,

deathlike sorrow, overwhelmed Him.

He invited three to stay with Him, speaking like a needy man,

rather than a needed man. they were to keep watch, to remain alert,

to give Him that moment.

He went farther into the dark heart of gethsemane and

fell face first in desperation.

He cried to Father

and asked for reprieve: "maybe there is another way. must I drink of the bitter cup?"

the words carried His brokenness, His turmoil;

they proved His pathos.

Jesus did not stop with His desire;

He refused to conclude after sobbing out His hope for an alternative.

"no matter, God, I will do as You see fit. carry out Your plan."

He rose from prayer, from blood, from sweat,

and returned to His watchmen.

He had given them a privileged charge. He found them sleeping.

He called them.

He coddled them, taught them, trained them. then He needed them

in a different way but they slept.

to peter, who was out like a rock, He offered a rebuke

tempered only by His exhaustion. "an hour isn't so much, is it?

only one hour and you cannot watch with Me,

watch for Me?

temptation will rob you unless you learn to watch and pray. the battle rages;

flesh so weak and spirit strong. feed your spirit.

do not satisfy the flesh."

a second time He cried to God in prayer. speaking the same words.

a second time He returned.

a second time He found His closest friends sleeping.

a third time He cried to God in prayer. speaking the same words.

a third time He returned.

a third time He found His closest friends sleeping.

how sad.

their sleepy refusal to spend the night in prayer when the Master solicited their participation. didn't they sense His hurt?

didn't they?

they didn't

fight off sleep to embrace prayer, to share pain. was it could not or would not?

am I different?

what replaces my prayer as sleep did theirs?

Jesus invited them to pray in the dark. they slept.

they never liked His talk of death anyway. maybe a restless nap

helped them escape the nagging awareness that He really was going away

soon.

years have passed since that dark night.

maybe He weeps even now at God's right hand. no tears in heaven?

can He see the child slapped by an impatient parent, the man battling an incurable disease,

the family on the brink of collapse, the killing of the innocent,
the laughter of the guilty,

the multitudes unmoved by His love?

can He see?

if He sees, He cries.

if He cries, He prays. always interceding.

if He sees and cries and prays, He calls us.

He invites us into the darkness of the garden.

spend the night with Him in crucial prayer. not

pleading for trinkets or hoping for fun.

now,

crying for Life and dying for Love.

tonight,

with the drum of destiny beating, beating, beating, close and clear,

can we watch one hour?

a bitter cup and a Father's will, temptation and tears, flesh and spirit.

at this time He cries out to God in prayer. at some time He will return.

will He find us sleeping?

READ:

Then Jesus went with his disciples to a place called Gethsemane, and he said to them, "Sit here while I go over there and pray." He took Peter and the two sons of Zebedee along with him, and he began to be sorrowful and troubled. Then he said to them, "My soul is overwhelmed with sorrow to the point of death. Stay here and keep watch with me."

Going a little farther, he fell with his face to the ground and prayed, "My Father, if it is possible, may this cup be taken from me. Yet not as I will, but as you will."

Then he returned to his disciples and found them sleeping. "Could you men not keep watch with me for one hour?" he asked Peter. "Watch and pray so that you will not fall into temptation. The spirit is willing, but the body is weak."

He went away a second time and prayed, "My Father, if it is not possible for this cup to be taken away unless I drink it, may your will be done."

When he came back, he again found them sleeping, because their eyes were heavy. So he left them and went away once more and prayed the third time, saying the same thing.

Then he returned to the disciples and said to them, "Are you still sleeping and resting? Look, the hour is near, and the Son of Man is betrayed into the hands of sinners. Rise, let us go! Here comes my betrayer!" (Matthew 26:36–45)

REFLECT:

1. When have you prayed such deep, painful, honest prayers?

2. Did any of your friends join you in your hurt?

3. How do you describe Christ's encounter that night?

4. What can you learn from His experience?

RECEIVE:

> Humanity is fickle. They may dress for a morning coronation and never feel the need to change clothes to attend an execution in the afternoon.
>
> So Triumphal Sundays and Good Fridays always fit comfortably into the same April week.
> —Calvin Miller[77]

RESPOND:

- Read this chapter again slowly.
- Take time to write a poetic narrative of the event.
- Or draw a picture.
- Or write a song.
- Use part of your artistic thinking to endure a healthy process of that painful evening of surrender.
- And choose to surrender in your own life.

---

77 Calvin Miller, *The Singer* (Downers Grove, IL: InterVarsity, 1975) 87.

28

The Dying

Matthew 27:45–46

The night stood dumb. The burdened mother
wept. "The Ancient Star-Song lost. The World
Hater won. I wish I might have died instead of
you, my son, my son, my son."
—Calvin Miller[78]

The week ended. The week merging celebration and
accusation ended.

Weeks do that. They begin their sprint then rush toward
a conclusion. Like stories, our weeks contain components of
drama and tension and conflict and romance and resolution.
To pause during our weeks indicates we notice the fragments,
we see the invisible, we imagine the wonder, we gaze beyond
the obvious. We believe. While doubting and questioning, we
choose to believe. When feeling nothing much at all, we believe.

Even when we watch a Hero punished.

---

78 Calvin Miller, *The Singer,* 119.

Even when we turn our back on our Hero.

Even when we hide, barely able to notice our Hero dying.

Even when the conflict and tension appear to indicate our selected Hero became the victim.

Christ's followers found themselves not sitting on our comfortable seats in the theater many years later. They weren't standing to sing a reverent song in remembrance of a distant holiday. They were there as it occurred. Their screen was real time. Their ears heard; their eyes saw; their emotions felt.

Their lives—risking all to pause and follow by chasing the dreams of a single figure in this drama—appeared to be ending also.

But we must pause here. We must not rush past this part of the story. If we revisit this scene often enough, if we taste the reminders of Holy Communion deeply enough, if we image the bloody depiction realistic enough, we let sacraments bring faith and hope and love. We allow death to fetch us life.

How? Because from the scene of Christ's cruel death comes a segment of this narrative that gives us deeper reason to pause, that offers us a larger purpose for mentally noticing all the wonder these pages have offered as realities in the present.

Here's what happened. Jesus suffered the agony of bloody, painful punishment. Crucified between two guilty convicts, a cross clutched a holy, hurting Body. Breaths were hard to absorb, to release. Swallowing wouldn't work right. Bones, muscles, skin: the trapped flesh faced a lock in the zone of realignment.

All parts found normal tasks almost impossible. His ears could hear, though. They could receive words spoken by the men on each side. His brain could interpret and understand the noise. Jesus knew the other observers made fun of Him.

Two criminals who were crucified on each side of Christ also heaped insults on Him.[79] Yet, the behavior of one of the two men soon changed. Drastically.

The dying criminal gained a view of his life's pages as he endured the last chapter while staring at Christ. He decided to respond differently than the man on the other side of Jesus. Their reactions reveal two extremes of perspective.

The ways we truly view ourselves rise above the surface during times of crisis. That was such a time for them. When the curtain began closing on their lives, the man to the left of Jesus and the man to the right of Jesus played the last acts in sharp contrasts. One played the role of pride. The other, humility.

Pride spoke with a curse and a mocking smile: "Prove yourself."

Humility cried with a hope and a dream: "Remember me."

The repentant thief voted Jesus as innocent, crying out through his pain: "This man has done nothing wrong." He then acknowledged himself as guilty, "We are getting punished justly. We deserve everything that is happening to us." When

---

79 Mark15:32

conclusions blend human wrong with divine righteousness, the results reveal respect for the Just God. The guilty man asked the one on the wrong side of Christ, "Don't you fear God?"

Conviction and repentance are not bad words. They are steps up from a basement of destruction. They are entrances to a new domain. They are requests for rescue, for help, for a need to be carried.

At the end of this thief's life he gained the proper perspective of what his life had been like. He was ready to move on in the drama of salvation.

Glance for a wider view now, though. See again the bigger picture. Soldiers watched, possessing regal weaponry and governmental authority. They appeared the most capable candidates of rescue. Instead of begging for mercy from them, however, that man called out to Jesus, One who shared his distress. The request? To deliver him from the agony of that moment, and to direct him in the journey ahead.

To receive assistance, the thief called upon the One who had been whipped, ridiculed, and humiliated, hanging beside him, dying beside him, suffocating slowly. The thief prayed, "Remember me."

If at such a low state Jesus can assist a desperate man, what can He do today for people like us? Maybe we should—if we hope for His help—offer a prayer as the thief did. And we must offer it with humility and expectancy.

The Dying

"Jesus, remember me." Notice the simplicity, the specifics. The next statement qualifies the time for the desired recollection: "When you come into your Kingdom."

We heard him address the other criminal, the man dying on the opposite side of Jesus. Then we heard words directed to Christ. Next, Jesus offered words. From His place of intense suffering, the crucified Christ responded to the thief's request, to his prayer. Jesus promised to help the man beside Him. Notice the progression of Christ's encouraging declaration: today. . . you will. . . be with Me. . . in paradise.

Think about an eternity of pausing with Jesus.

And think about how it doesn't just begin when these old bodies end their jobs. Merge this story with all the other stories of Jesus. Time with Him is a part of each day, each encounter, each breath.

That lifestyle gives us deeper hope about when we breathe no more.

That assurance gives us realistic optimism as we breathe in the moment.

Well, speaking of moments, Good Friday ended. Christ died. According to biblical teaching, that is what He had to do for us.

He was taken away and placed in a safe location—like a cave covered for protection.

Not sure what happened in that room, but it wasn't the planned agenda. The story wasn't over and the movie hadn't ended.

More was about to happen. More noise and tension, more conflict and resolution, more drama and surprise.

And that's where we will finish for now. With a pause as we glance back in time. Peeking into an empty tomb and realizing our beliefs are real, our statements of faith are true, our story ends will, let's just pause.

Let's take a deep breath and give thanks.

That weekend was a new beginning.

READ:

> One of the criminals who hung there hurled insults at him: "Aren't you the Christ? Save yourself and us!"
>
> But the other criminal rebuked him. "Don't you fear God," he said, "since you are under the same sentence? We are punished justly, for we are getting what our deeds deserve. But this man has done nothing wrong."
>
> Then he said, "Jesus, remember me when you come into your kingdom."

Jesus answered him, "I tell you the truth, today you will be with me in paradise."
(Luke 23:39–43)

REFLECT:

1. What thoughts and feelings come to you as you read this story of Christ's death?

2. What part of the story hurts you the most?

3. What is Christ saying to you through this story?

4. How do you plan to respond?

RECEIVE:

Over against that terrible word of despair the Lord of history flung the word, "Emmanuel" (God with us). Morning had broken, and Sunday shouts that Saturday is over; the shackles have been busted and our human condition has been finally and conclusively answered

in grace. Grace incarnate, that steps out of the valley of the shadow of death and announces, "I am he that was dead, and behold I am alive forever more."
—Donald L. Gokee[80]

RESPOND:

- Receive the Communion elements.
- Sit in silence.
- Read the story from Good Friday to Resurrection Day.
- Celebrate the story.
- Proclaim, "He is risen; He is risen indeed."

80 Donald L. Gokee, *It's a Love-Haunted World* (Lima, OH: C.S.S. Publishing Co. Inc., 1985) 98.

29

The Breakfast

John 21:25

In the meanwhile, he had much to do and far to go, he said, and so did she, and the first thing she did was go back to the disciples to report. "I have seen the Lord," she said, and whatever dark doubts they might have had on the subject earlier, one look at her face was enough to melt them all away like morning mist. —Frederick Buechner[81]

Breakfast is my friend.

Breakfast moments remind me of life, of new beginnings, of community, of pausing to eat and talk and think and begin a day. I cherish the morning meals. That honest conversation I enjoyed last week with Charles when we met for breakfast at the Roystonian. That drive through a storm to meet my friend Tom for breakfast in Atlanta before I flew to Orlando and he flew to

---

81 Frederick Buechner, *Peculiar Treasures,* 103.

Japan. That breakfast of questions and ideas as I sat with Greg. That breakfast with Tim as we enjoyed a Saturday together in the neighborhood I had lived in for many years but left almost a decade before than morning. Those many breakfasts of my young years before Mama moved to breakfast in heaven. Those many breakfasts watching our three sons grow up. Those breakfasts over many years in many places with many friends and family members. These healthy breakfasts I eat most mornings alone when home and up very early to write and pray and think.

Each breakfast, I believe, can welcome Jesus.

Even when He seems far, far away.

Maybe, that's how His followers felt after He died.

The fishermen-turned-disciples felt disillusioned. Jesus never established a Kingdom on earth. At least, not the way His followers expected He would. For all His talk, His walk, and His amazing miracles, they had little practical proof of prophetic phrases Christ linked to Himself. From a crowd of seekers to crucifixion by public opinion. From water into wine to a bloody death. His closest friends dropped into doubt as their dreams dashed. Wasn't Christ supposed to be seated on David's throne? Had their three years of missionary service done anything at all?

Peter, as usual, got things rolling. However his friends felt, he decided to move on. And, as usual, he made his decision public: "I'm going fishing." Others joined him. They climbed back into a boat to fish, sitting in the setting where Jesus had found them before. With tarnished dreams, they returned to their lives before Christ. They went fishing.

The Breakfast

Watching multitudes dwindle down to just a few discouraged the disciples. It challenged their plan to change the world. Their own cowardice showed during the days of Christ's death. It shook their beliefs. Tired of risks, they launched in a boat driven by goals easily attainable and measurable.

More was happening though. Christ's death had not ended the story. A weekend of pain ended with an empty tomb, beginning a season inviting everyone everywhere to receive love from Jesus. He revealed Himself to a few—never notifying them in advance of His arrival. He talked to Peter about the future, talked to Thomas about doubt, and talked to all His followers about why He must leave again.

But He didn't give specific details.

I like specific details, advance notice, clear guidance, and precise goals to achieve. Jesus chose to voice a general agenda—like love one another, wait, receive the Spirit, and tell the story.

He still seems to lead that way.

And, amid crucial times to achieve aspirations, He waits for us. With our boats running and our goals listed, He waits for us. Cooking us breakfast.

That's what happened for His early followers.

The disciples—or, for now, the fishermen—had worked through the night but caught nothing. Jesus waited ashore and spoke, possibly making the apparent disaster of the disciples worse. He advised them on a better fishing technique.

Remember, they'd been there a while. They'd tried it all and they had been fishermen for years. They probably didn't want an outsider's advice.

Jesus told them to try the right side. They proceeded without hesitation. They still did not know the Lord's identity, but maybe eager Peter learned a lesson the first time Jesus directed them to a large catch. Maybe he figured it was worth a shot. So, they lowered their net, following the Stranger's guidelines. The shifted net suddenly filled with fish.

They could not bring in the net because of captured quantity. They didn't need to make up a story about a miracle at sea. What a great illustration of Christ's power, His wisdom, His guidance, His awareness. Utilizing years of education and experience, the efforts of men brought nothing. When their work followed the advice of Jesus, success was immediate.

I often see how we abandon our ideals and return to the roles we are most comfortable with. The preaching, healing, and traveling may have seemed too much for the less-than-perfect disciples. Fishing posed no problems. They knew technique; they felt confident about their abilities.

Can't we all relate?

To encourage them to fulfill the call, Jesus did not rebuke them. Through an amazing miracle He revealed His power. He opted for showing Himself to them rather than shoving Himself on them. Not volume. Not marketing. Harsh words might have added to their despair. The miracle, reminiscent of the similar episode so long before,[82] taught the lesson.

Stare at John's words: "It is the Lord!" His spoken excitement compelled Simon Peter to act. With no desire to conceal his enthusiasm, Peter wrapped his outer garment, dove into the water and traveled the hundred yards like an Olympic swimmer. Peter forgot the fish. His mind was on Jesus. He let the coworkers row in the harvest. He rushed to see his friend. When the boat arrived, Peter reached to drag ashore the net bulging with proof of Christ's promise.

It really was the Lord. They saw Him. He was there. Alive and with them. Peter's eager plunge showed a longing to be with the Savior. Jesus gladly gave him that opportunity.

On the shore they found coals warm and bread ready. They gazed at their Host and knew, for certain, Jesus had invited them to eat.

He gave them what they thought they needed: a catch of fish. But He gave it on His terms, not theirs. He gave them what their bodies needed: food. He prepared it. He served it. Even more crucial, He gave them what they truly needed in the deepest place of their lives: He gave them Himself.

Jesus offered not even a small rebuke. A Chef on the verge of clarifying Peter's pastoral commission, He shared Himself. A ministry that began in an encounter with men fishing took its

---

82 Luke 5:1–11

realignment to that familiar bargaining table. The staff felt like giving up, like quitting. Their CEO crashed their pity-party and loved them.

All of us are tempted to retreat to safe, secure, more familiar places when initial thrills wane. When we feel too many prayers remain unanswered and too much effort goes unnoticed, we glance around in search of a way out. When pressures of ministry push us to the brink of burn out, we settle for a more comfortable to the flesh, less demanding or challenging role.

The Holy Observer watches us when we sail the boats of resignation. Whether we intend to back off permanently or just in moments of uncertainty, He watches our every move. He knows our every motive. And He loves us.

That's what Jesus does. He shows up. He glances from the shore as we labor in our efforts to escape. He comes to host us at the breakfast table. He meets us right where we are, even in our weakest moments.

His table waits. The Host has invited us who are still in our boats to ride ashore, or dive in and swim to Him.

He says, "Let's eat."

READ:

> Afterward Jesus appeared again to his disciples, by the Sea of Galilee. It happened this way: Simon Peter, Thomas (called Didymus), Nathanael from Cana in Galilee, the sons of Zebedee, and two other disciples

were together. "I'm going out to fish," Simon Peter told them, and they said, "We'll go with you." So they went out and got into the boat, but that night they caught nothing.

Early in the morning, Jesus stood on the shore, but the disciples did not realize that it was Jesus.

He called out to them, "Friends, haven't you any fish?"

"No," they answered.

He said, "Throw your net on the right side of the boat and you will find some." When they did, they were unable to haul the net in because of the large number of fish.

Then the disciple whom Jesus loved said to Peter, "It is the Lord!" As soon as Simon Peter heard him say, "It is the Lord," he wrapped his outer garment around him (for he had taken it off) and jumped into the water. The other disciples followed in the boat, towing the net full of fish, for they were not far from shore, about a hundred yards. When they landed, they saw a fire of burning coals there with fish on it, and some bread.

Jesus said to them, "Bring some of the fish you have just caught."

Simon Peter climbed aboard and dragged the net ashore. It was full of large fish, 153, but even with so many the net was not torn. Jesus said to them, "Come and have breakfast." None of the disciples dared ask him, "Who are you?" They knew it was the Lord. Jesus came, took the bread and gave it to them, and did the same with the fish. This was now the third time Jesus appeared to his disciples after he was raised from the dead (John 21:1–14).

REFLECT:

1. How do you think the disciples felt?

2. How have you responded when you felt alone and far from Christ?

3. Imagine having a breakfast with Him.

RECEIVE:

Once more Jesus paused. He glanced down at the nail marks in His wrists before turning to Peter one final time. A third time. "Simon, son of John, do you love Me?" —Karen Kingsbury[83]

RESPOND:

- Imagine meeting Jesus for breakfast.
- Think of coming on the shore, hearing Jesus saying, "Come."
- He is inviting you toward Himself. How will you respond?

83 Karen Kingsbury, *The Friends of Jesus* (Brentwood, TN: Howard Books, 2015) 179.

30

The Noise

Matthew 28:16–20

> Taken alone, each work is good; but taken
> together as a series, each part gains fuller
> meaning as we see it in relation to the bigger
> idea being explored. So it is with Christian
> community. Each one of us is a work of art;
> but together we tell an even greater story.
> —Bob Kilpatrick and Joel Kilpatrick[84]

Do you hear the noise?

Jesus leaving earth so His people could change the world. An odd strategy, wouldn't you think?

But God planned to let His presence dwell within His people. They could—as we now can—pause and be with Jesus through a Spirit called Holy. The world has never been the same.

Do you hear the noise?

---

84 Bob Kilpatrick and Joel Kilpatrick, *The Art of Being You*, 64–65.

They, the people in that time and place as we read in Acts chapter 2, heard the noise.

Throughout the stories of the early church, the noise was heard. Of revival and healing. Of prisons opening. Of persecution and boats, of odd conversations and a persecutor becoming a leader of the persecuted ones. Of Stephen preaching the message of Jesus even when the audience attempted to silence him by pummeling him with stones. Stephen looked toward the heavens. He saw his Hope standing at God's right hand ready to welcome him home.

Throughout the stories of the church over the years and around the world, the noise has been heard. Sounds of prayers voiced in praise and in desperation. Sounds of requests lifted in faith and in doubt. Sounds of God's love outside of cathedrals and into homes—homes of a families, homes of friends, homes of enemies.

I often hear the noise in groups—small and large groups, young and old people—as they gather together in their similar goals and styles and order of services.

But as I pause with Jesus and read more about the time after Christ's ascension, I think of other sounds I crave to hear. Let's not see this as the church of my personal makeup, my preferred style of worship, my tribe, my grouping, my club, the place where I fit in.

Over the last few decades I've dreamed of the ideal local church. The Chris preference of a quality building design and modern technical equipment and astounding talent is what I want. That, though, is not what I need. That, though, doesn't seem to match what Jesus would craft.

Imagine a place not crafted just for one nationality, one age group, one language. A place not including just one musical style, one preaching style, one liturgical style. A place not ruled by one design, one visionary leader, one trend.

But a place welcoming many skin colors, languages, and styles. A place not labeling itself as the church, but letting people know that it's just a building to offer everybody everywhere a place to call home and be healed so they can be sent out to bring others into the *Pause with Jesus* lifestyle. A family and a place aiming to welcome people with Cerebral palsy, Down syndrome, muscular dystrophy, multiple sclerosis, epilepsy, autism, hard of hearing, hard to remember, spinal bifida, depression, bipolar, traumatic brain injuries, blind, addictions, anxiety, personality disorder, sleep disorder, eating disorder, and other hidden weaknesses that often keep people distant from churches.

A place choosing to give up the loud noises which damage our ears, to use sign language for those who cannot hear, to build chairs which are comfortable and movable—out of the way for groups to gather and out of the way to make room for wheelchairs. A place of regular communion—traditionally and creatively helping us remember the cost to enter. A place of art, music, drama, silence, reverence. A place of learning to read, learning to learn, learning to be forgiven, learning to be set free from addictions. A place grasping church history deeper than the life of one demonization or trend or culture, but a larger tribe declaring ancient prayers and honoring historical readings and hearing from leaders whose voices are distant in time but so near in spirit.

And more than a place. People. A family. People of many languages and many ages and many backgrounds. People who think and live this way: inclusive people, inclusive God, inclusive thinking, inclusive ministry, inclusive language, inclusive church life, inclusive buildings. A place and a family which has decided to think and live this way: including people with learning disabilities, including people with autism, including people with sight loss, including people with hearing loss, including people with mobility difficulty, including people with mental health conditions, including families with children who have additional needs.[85]

Do you hear the noise?

Where the individual who processes slowly isn't ignored or fired for their lack of leadership skills. Where the individual who hasn't ever been free from an addiction is loved so much that they take a few steps they've never been willing to take before. Where the person unable to drive because of epilepsy sees a line of volunteers ready to drive her home. Where the person unable to bathe on his own because of multiple health issues sees a line of volunteers ready to make him clean. Where the

---

85 For more information, see Tony Phelps-Jones, et al., *Making Church Accessible to All: Including Disabled People in Church Life* (Abingdon, UK: The Bible Reading Fellowship, 2013).

visionary team sees more than *goals to reach* but *people to love.* Where the stage no longer includes the trendy and expensive lighting because the family finally realizes the danger to family members with brain injuries. Where offerings are not only taken but given away. Where the young man with Down syndrome is allowed to lead the congregation in a song he can't sing the way approved vocalists would sing it. Where the pastor loves the parishioners and the stories and the people who don't like him at all. Where the pastor's wife doesn't feel a need to perform, but to love and be loved just as she is. Where the scholarly attendee decides to not analyze a simple sermon but realizes the words were just what he needed. Where the uneducated attendee senses a new inspiration to dive deep into study and research as ways of spending time with Jesus. Where preachers of two different theological circles choose to go to the same restaurant after the service ends and, instead of debating, take food to serve a homeless man together. Where politicians of opposing parties find a better way to party together, refusing to let differences of opinions and policies rob them of being a family of a Father, a Son, and a Spirit. Where people are welcomed and accepted, mentored and guided, taught and heard, forgiven and dared to dream again.

Jesus seems to enjoy that church.

Don't you see Him there?

Can you see yourself there?

Writing this feels like a Kingdom coming, like a Father's will being done, like a church of whosoever will, like a motto of everybody everywhere, like the beatitudes in real time, like the epistle of James taken seriously, like the book of Acts continuing her chronicle, like realizing that how we treat others is actually how we are treating Jesus, like His church instead of my church, like Revelation becoming a reality.

Others tell me that's how it will be in heaven. Others tell me that's just my dream and not a possibility in our world of division, discrimination, denominations, and people-pleasing motives. Others tell me that's not practical because everybody needs to fit with their own tribe.

I get their points.

But another part of me, or another Voice to me, inspires me to think wild thoughts and dream passionate dreams. I see Jesus in the middle of my imagined church building. I envision a smile on His face as He sits on the floor in the middle of a row of attendees on their wheelchairs. I hear Him singing loudly then softly, dancing a little then being still a little, looking at each face and letting every person see His love through those eyes. I notice those eyes becoming wet as He stares toward an image of a globe and His mind begins to focus on people who say they hate Him while His heart still yearns to sing them a love song.

I continue to hear noise and see through glasses of hope. Hope of God sightings in common life being a part of every church in every tribe. Hope of bathrooms designed to make my friends in wheelchairs comfortable there. Hope of ramps to enter a stage so those same wheelchairs are welcome toward the center of attention. Hope of prayers being prayed, help being offered, medical and psychological care being encouraged, and neighborhoods knowing "love your neighbors" and "love your enemies" and "how you treat others is really how you treat Jesus" as purpose statements of the church.

I pause and imagine. I realize the order of service is not designed to meet my own objectives or to fit my preferred style. I relish the joyful reverence and the noisy silence. I appreciate the mixture of colors and ages and styles and stories. I sense an awe, a fear, a peace, a welcoming surprise. I comprehend, though still very slightly, a glimpse at the bigger picture, the larger story, the kingdom and the power and the glory.

Do you hear the noise?

To pause with Jesus is invading a voyage of transformation. One story, one sentence, one day, one breath, one moment at a time. Beside a few, among a crowd, alone in silence. In a boat, beside a well, on a tree, in the water. Being baptized, being tempted, being crucified, being alive again. Saying hello and saying goodbye. An entrance and a departure. An apprentice. A lover. Laughter and tears. A cross and an empty tomb. A dove and a fire. Yesterday and tomorrow.

All so real in the moment. In this moment. Letting the story of Jesus invade our stories and shift the end of a narrative toward recovery and redemption and rest.

Listen to the noise of an invitation.

Pause.

With Jesus.

Today.

And forever.

But get ready. The whole world just might hear the noise.

READ:

> They devoted themselves to the apostles' teaching and to fellowship, to the breaking of bread and to prayer. Everyone was filled with awe at the many wonders and signs performed by the apostles. All the believers were together and had everything in common. They sold property and possessions to give to anyone who had need. Every day they continued to meet together in the temple courts. They broke bread in their homes and ate together with glad and sincere hearts, praising God and enjoying the favor of all the people. And the Lord added to their number daily those who were being saved (Acts 2:42–47).

REFLECT:

1. What story from the book of Acts inspires you?

2. What part of this chapter's image of church challenges you? Why?

3. How does God want you to change and become more like Jesus?

4. Will you?

RECEIVE:

> If we want to experience the deep love of Jesus, we enter into loving him—directly, through prayer and meditation on his word, and indirectly, by loving others, especially those who struggle or suffer.
> —Keri Wyatt Kent[86]

RESPOND:

- Write your own version of the "church" described in this chapter.
- List practical ways you can change to make this big dream a reality in your own world.
- Pray Christ's body becomes one.
- Do what you can to make it happen with His love.

---

86 Keri Wyatt Kent, *Deeply Loved*, 93.

Conclusion: To Stay

> All I needed to do was apologize, but I had to argue. All I needed to do was listen, but I had to open my big mouth. All I needed to do was be patient, but I had to take control. All I needed to do was give it to God, but I tried to fix it myself. —Max Lucado[87]

"You ever gonna write a book that's not about Jesus? I'm just not into reading this stuff."

I thanked my new friend for his honesty. But I didn't know how to answer his question.

If he was asking if I would write a book that doesn't cover pages with specific details about biblical stories and doesn't clearly emphasize the name of Jesus, then I guess the answer is yes. I like to write about many aspects of life. Some of our future book plans might not quote Scripture or use biblical narratives as the guide.

But if he wants me to tell stories without Jesus on my mind or in my heart, without Jesus guiding the overall goals, and

---

87 Max Lucado, *Traveling Light*, 23.

without Jesus helping the weak man that I am, the answer is no. I'm not trying to sound preachy or holy or good or like a saint. And that's really my point. I'm not holy or good or a saint, and the only preaching I can really do is to say that Christ is my goodness, Christ is my holiness, Christ is the saint who has found a way to invade the life of a weak dreamer like me.

Anyway, I tried to explain my true self to my new friend. No one else was around and he didn't seem eager to purchase any of my books, so we took turns telling stories. He told me a few surface stories and we laughed. Before our time ended he told me a deep, honest, painful story and we cried.

He said, "I don't even know you and I don't like all this Jesus talk. But here I am telling you what I don't want to tell you. And I'm crying. I don't know what's wrong. I never cry."

I listened and cried. He left, walking to the restroom as other attendees walked toward my booth.

The ancient accounts from the eastern world appeared near as I read them again and wrote these stories. My heart seemed to beat differently. My soul felt loved. My self-talk changed channels. The *me that I am* surrendered in new ways to *the me being mentored by Christ.*

Stories from the past became alive in the present. Characters from the Bible's pages felt like creatures in the now. Christ's invitations, stories, questions, and silence emerged here—right here, right now.

The meditative exchange in *Pause with Jesus* lured me toward a healthy perspective, an unexpected welcome, a relationship based on unconditional love, a sacrifice—on a new collection of words so different from our typical thoughts about ourselves and our importance. We don't need to prove or perform, succeed or achieve, rehearse our elevator speeches or edit our lives before He smiles and invites us in.

He is smiling and inviting already.

He is crying and caring already.

He is near. Not distant, but here.

But isn't there a waiting list to stand or sit beside Him? Isn't there a dress code? Isn't there a proper vocabulary? Isn't there a trick that only a few culturally successful minds remember?

No.

Just Him. Inviting us.

Now.

He says the cost is covered. He assures us we are allowed to enter.

My friend from the conference did return after dinner. Not crying. Actually looking like a different man. Other guests had left my booth so it was just us again.

But as he talked about Jesus this time—with a different tone than I'd heard from his voice earlier, with more of a smile than I'd seen on his face earlier—he sounded like a healed man. He stayed a long time. The anger and hurt and inner scars didn't seem to be in charge this time. As we talked about possible ideas for him to gain the best lens to see life, he was nodding instead of shaking his head. He had a little hope after crying away a few drops of his past. Our plan offered ways for him to visit Jesus in everyday life and to obtain appropriate friends to join him in the journey.

I realized that maybe it wasn't just us after all.

Jesus seemed to have paused and came over to love my new friend. And to stay.

And to me, that is the story. For my new friend, for Jesus, for you, for me, for us.

The story that will really never end.

> One of the greatest paradoxes of the Gospel is that surrender is victory. —Brennan Manning[88]

> With the Holy Spirit resting upon us as Jesus promised, our part is to host the very presence of God wherever we are, to exercise the very power of God in every situation and to witness the gospel and what God has done in Jesus and is doing in the world today. —Os Guinness[89]

> The Lord Jesus then pours out the Holy Spirit to form the holy People of God, a community of prophets and lovers who will surrender to

---

88 Brennan Manning, *The Relentless Tenderness of Jesus* (Revell, 2004) 68.
89 Os Guinness, *Fool's Talk: Recovering the Art of Christian Persuasion* (Downers Grove, IL: InterVarsity Press, 2015) 59.

the mystery of the fire of the Spirit than burns within, who will live in ever greater fidelity to the shattering, omnipresent Word, who will enter into the center of all that is, into the very heart and mystery of God, into the center of that flame that consumes and purifies and sets all aglow with peace, joy, boldness, and extravagant love. —Brennan Manning[90]

"The Church's One Foundation"

by Samuel J. Stone, 1839–1900

Stanza 1.

The Church's one foundation

    Is Jesus Christ, her Lord;

She is His new creation

    By water and the Word.

    From heaven He came and sought her

    To be His holy bride;

With His own blood He bought her,

    And for her life He died.

Stanza 2.

Elect from every nation,

---

90 Brennan Manning, *The Importance of Being Foolish: How to Think Like Jesus* (San Francisco: HarperSanFransico, 2005) 43.

Yet one o'er all the earth,
Her charter of salvation

One Lord, one faith, one birth.
One holy name she blesses,

Partakes one holy food,
And to one hope she presses,

With every grace endued.
Stanza 3.

The Church shall never perish!

Her dear Lord, to defend,
To guide, sustain, and cherish,

Is with her to the end.
Though there be those that hate her.

False sons within her pale,
Against both foe and traitor

She ever shall prevail.
Stanza 4.

Though with a scornful wonder

Men see her sore oppressed,
By schisms rent asunder,

By heresies distressed,

Yet saints their watch are keeping;

 Their cry goes up, "How long?"

And soon the night of weeping

 Shall be the morn of song.

Stanza 5.

Mid toil and tribulation

 And tumult of her war

She waits the consummation

 Of peace forevermore,

'Til with the vision glorious

 Her longing eyes are blest

And the great Church victorious

 Shall be the Church at rest.

About the Author

Chris Maxwell is a pastor, speaker, and author. He knows about struggles and weaknesses, and about joy and hope. He is thankful for his wife, Debbie, their three sons—Taylor and Aaron and Graham—and all their other relatives and friends.

Invite Chris to speak to your group about his life with Jesus, his years of pastoring, his love of stories, or his life-changing illness.

Follow Chris on Facebook and Twitter, order his books on Amazon or other places, and visit his website www.chrismaxwell.me.